LEARNINGEXPRESS BASIC SKILLS

CRITICAL THINKING AND LOGIC SKILLS
FOR COLLEGE STUDENTS

CRITICAL THINKING AND LOGIC SKILLS

FOR COLLEGE STUDENTS

Elizabeth Chesla

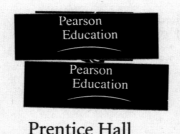

Pearson
Education

Pearson
Education

Prentice Hall

Library of Congress Cataloging-in-Publication Data

Chesla, Elizabeth L.
    Critical thinking and logic skills for college students / by Elizabeth L. Chesla
        p.   cm.—(LearningExpress basic skills for college)
    ISBN 0–13–082838–6
    1. Critical thinking—Study and teaching (Higher) 2. Study skills. 3. Logic
    I. Title. II. Title: Critical thinking and logic skills for college students. III. Series.
LB2395.35.C54   1999
378.1'7'0281—DC21

98–26091
CIP

Acquisitions Editor: *Sue Bierman*
Managing Editor: *Mary Carnis*
Director of Manufacturing & Production: *Bruce Johnson*
Manufacturing Buyer: *Marc Bove*
Editorial Assistant: *Michelle M. Williams*

© 1999 by LearningExpress, LLC.
Published by Prentice Hall, Inc.
Simon & Schuster/A Viacom Company
Upper Saddle River, New Jersey 07458

Printed in the United States of America
10 9 8 7 6 5 4 3 2 1

ISBN: 0–13–082838–6

Prentice Hall International (UK) Limited, *London*
Prentice Hall of Australia Pty. Limited, *Sydney*
Prentice Hall of Canada Inc., *Toronto*
Prentice Hall Hispanoamericana, S.A., *Mexico*
Prentice Hall of India Private Limited, *New Delhi*
Prentice Hall of Japan, Inc., *Tokyo*
Simon & Schuster Asia Pte. Ltd., *Singapore*
Editora Prentice Hall do Brasil, Ltda., *Rio de Janeiro*

OTHER TITLES FROM PRENTICE HALL

New Beginnings: A Guide for Adult Learners and Returning Students (Simon) ISBN 0-13-849605-6

Frame by Frame: A Visual Guide to College Success (Lowenstein/Todd) ISBN 0-13-891268-8

The Distance Learner's Guide: Navigating the Collegiate Information Highway (Western Cooperative for Educational Telecommunications) ISBN 0-13-939513-X

Keys to Success, brief edition (Carter/Bishop/Kravits) ISBN 0-13-010798-8

Keys to Success 2/e (Carter/Bishop/Kravits) ISBN 0-13-861089-4

Keys to Effective Learning (Carter/Bishop/Kravits) ISBN 0-13-632191-7

Student Resource Guide to the Internet: Student Success Online (Leshin) ISBN 0-13-621079-1

Urban Learners: Serious About Success (DeLucia) 2/e ISBN 0-13-95963-3

Life Transitions (DiMarco) ISBN 0-13-776931-8

Building Self-Esteem: Strategies for Success in School and Beyond 2/e (Golden/Lesh) ISBN 0-13-776899-0

Academic Alternatives: Exploration and Decision Making 4/e (Gordon/Sears) ISBN 0-13-777715-9

Is This Going to be on the Test? And Ten Other Questions That Can Save Your College Career 3/e (Majors/Yamasaki) ISBN 0-13-776741-2

College Success (Moore/Baker/Packer) ISBN 0-13-527391-9

Life Management: Skills for Busy People (Walters/McKee) ISBN 0-13-227539-2

The Career Fitness Program 5/e (Sukiennik/Bendat/Raufman) ISBN 0-13-780826-7

Career Development: A 21st Century Job Search Handbook 3/e (Breidenbach) ISBN 0-13-576588-9

The Career Tool Kit 2/e (Carter/Izumo) ISBN 0-13-754359-X

Keys to Career Success (Carter/Ozee/Bollinger) ISBN 0-13-834277-6

Resume Writing Made Easy 6/e (Coxford) ISBN 0-13-679853-5

Career Development by Design (Hanna) ISBN 0-13-527383-8

Career Focus: A Personal Job Search Guide 2/e (Lamarre) ISBN 0-13-748989-7

Making Career Decisions That Count (Luzzo) ISBN 0-13-777731-0

Building Your Career: A Guide to Your Future 2/e (Sears/Gordon) ISBN 0-13-780800-3

Graduating into the Nineties (Carter/June) ISBN 0-13-911207-3

Career Transitions (DiMarco) ISBN 0-13-776915-6

Hired! The Job Hunting/Life Planning Guide (Harris) ISBN 0-13-226812-4

Managing Career Transitions: Your Career as a Work in Progress (Hayes) ISBN 0-13-776782-X

The Career Adventure: Your Guide to Personal Assessment, Career Exploration, and Decision Making 2/e (Johnston) ISBN 0-13-080188-7

The Job Searcher's Handbook (Robbins) ISBN 0-13-199621-5

Keys to Workplace (Bishop/Izumo/Cole) ISBN 0-13-914086-7

Keys to Success Reader (Bishop/Wheeler) ISBN 0-13-010799-9

Majors Exploration (Bradbury/Reeves) ISBN 0-13-011379-4

Achieving Your Full Potential (Drown) ISBN 0-13-95681-4

Transition Into Business (The Darla Moore Shcool of Business–USC) ISBN 0-13-081541-1

Turning Points: The Career Guide for the New Century (Ducat) ISBN 0-13-727702-4

Job Search Navigator (Henderson/Adamson) ISBN 0-13-917907-0

ACKNOWLEDGEMENTS

We would like to thank the following people for reviewing the Basic Skills for College series. These books are better as a result of their time and effort:

Adrian Cloete, DeVry Institute of Technology—Irving

Thomas R. Gier, Ph.D., University of Alaska—Anchorage

Karan Hancock Gier, Ph.D., University of Alaska—Anchorage

Maureen Hurley, University of Missouri—Kansas City

Jon A. Schlenker, University of Maine—Augusta

Nancy Stegall, DeVry Institute of Technology—Phoenix

Very special thanks for their efforts go to Jan Gallagher, James Gish, and Barry Lippman at LearningExpress. Their efforts and those of their staff were essential and invaluable in making this series successful.

We appreciate the hours of diligent work of those at Prentice Hall: Mary Carnis, Marc Bove, Santos Shih, Rit Dojny, Dave Jagger, Julio Cassanelli, Sue Bierman, Carol Carter, Jeff McIlroy, Barbara Rosenberg, Michelle Williams, and Amy Diehl.

LearningExpress Basic Skills for College

Build basic skills *fast!* Each book offers essential tips and techniques plus plenty of practice exercises in critical skill areas. Ideal for beginning college students who need to brush up on the basics. A must for those who need to polish the skills that lead to success.

Math Skills for College Students (ISBN 0-13-080257-3)
Reading Skills for College Students (ISBN 0-13-080258-1)
Vocabulary & Spelling Skills for College Students (ISBN 0-13-080255-7)
Writing Skills for College Students (ISBN 0-13-080256-5)
Critical Thinking and Logic Skills for College Students (ISBN 0-13-082838-6)

CONTENTS

HOW TO USE THIS BOOK

This book is designed to help you improve your critical thinking and reasoning skills in lessons that only take a short amount of time each day to complete. If you read the chapters carefully and do all the exercises, you should see dramatic improvement in your ability to think critically and solve problems logically by the time you reach Lesson 20.

Although each lesson is designed to be an effective skill builder on its own, it is important that you proceed through this book in order, from Lesson 1 through Lesson 20. Like most other skills, critical thinking and reasoning develop in layers. Each lesson in this book builds upon the ideas discussed in those before it.

Each lesson provides several exercises that allow you to practice the skills you learn throughout the book. You'll find answers and explanations for these practice exercises to help you be sure you're on the right track. Each lesson also provides practical suggestions for how to continue practicing these skills throughout the rest of the day and week—and the rest of your life. In addition, two special review lessons go over the key skills and concepts in each half of the book and give you practice applying them in both academic and real-life situations.

To help you gauge your progress, this book starts with a pretest. You should take this pretest *before* you start Lesson 1. Then, after you've finished Lesson 20, take the post-test. The tests are different but comparable, so you will be able to see just how much your critical thinking and reasoning skills have improved from your studies.

BE AN ACTIVE LISTENER AND OBSERVER

To make the most of this text, it's important to remember that critical thinking and reasoning skills touch just about every aspect of life—personal, professional, academic, even spiritual. That's why it's so important to build these skills. You can begin building these skills right away by becoming an *active listener and observer*.

People often make mistakes and miss opportunities because they come to conclusions based on what they think or feel rather than on the *evidence* before them. They make decisions based on what they *want* to hear rather than what is really being said; they take action based on what they *imagine* to be true rather than what is actually the case. But by really listening to what people say and *how* they say it (facial expressions and tone of voice often say much more than words themselves), you help ensure that you will be reacting to what's really being said, not just what you want to hear.

Similarly, by paying attention and noticing things around you, you'll help ensure that the decisions you make and the conclusions you come to will be justified. For example, if a place feels unsafe to you, what is it about that place that makes you uncomfortable? Feelings generally come from things we are able to sense, even subconsciously, in our environment. The more you can see and point to as evidence for your thoughts, feelings, and actions, the more logical your decisions and actions will be.

Much of this book will be devoted to helping you build your observation skills. Meanwhile, here are a few pointers to help you not only as you work through this book but in everything you do.

KEEP AN OPEN MIND

It is very rarely the case that there is only *one* possible answer to a problem or only *one* "right" way to think or act. Even in math, where things seem to be black and white, there are always many ways to solve a problem. When it comes to making decisions, especially those that involve other people, remember that between black and white, there are a thousand shades of gray. You may prefer one shade over another, but that doesn't mean the other colors can't also be valid.

CONSIDER ALL SIDES

People often make the mistake of coming to a conclusion or making a decision before listening to or considering all sides of an argument. Similarly, problems are often amplified when looked at from only one perspective. That's why it is important to get as complete a picture you can get of a given situation; the more complete the picture, the more effective your decision or solution will be. Listen to all sides of an argument; look at a situation from various points of view. If you do, your decisions will be much more sound and you'll be able to solve problems more effectively.

SEPARATE FEELINGS FROM FACTS

This book will talk in more detail about the difference between fact and opinion later on, but the distinction is so important that it's worth mentioning now. What most often clouds people's ability to reason effectively is their emotions. It is natural, of course, to be led by emotions, but when you let feelings overwhelm your sense of reason, you often end up making poor decisions. This is not to say that you shouldn't consider your feelings—of course you should—but just be sure they're not overriding the facts.

THINK BEFORE YOU ACT

People are often under pressure to make quick decisions. But with the exception of emergency situations, it's usually best to take some time to reason things through. Hasty decisions are less productive in the long run because they're usually not the most logical or informed decisions. If you take a little time to think things through—to consider all sides and separate feelings from facts—you're much more likely to make a wise decision or find an effective solution.

Of course, sometimes making a quick decision is the only option, like when you're taking a timed test or in an emergency situation. That's why it's so important to build your reasoning skills now and make them a part of your everyday thought process. Then when you are pressed for time, you'll be able to reason through the situation quickly and effectively.

If any of this sounds confusing, don't worry—each of these ideas will be explained thoroughly in the lessons that follow. What's important is that you work on developing these skills as best as you can, starting with Lesson 1, "Critical Thinking and Reasoning Skills."

PRETEST

Before you start your study of reasoning skills, you may want to get an idea of how much you already know and how much you need to learn. If that's the case, take the pretest in this chapter.

The pretest consists of 35 multiple-choice questions covering all the lessons in this book. Naturally, not all of the reasoning skills in this book are covered on the test. Even if you get all of the questions on the pretest right, you will undoubtedly profit from working through the lessons anyway. On the other hand, if you miss a lot of questions on the pretest, don't despair. These lessons are designed to teach you critical thinking and reasoning skills step by step; take your time and enjoy the learning process.

So use this pretest just to get a general idea of how much of what's in this book you already know. If you get a high score on this pretest, you may be able to spend less time with this book than you originally planned. If you get a low score, you may find that you will need a little more time than you'd expected to get through each chapter and learn all about logical reasoning.

There's an answer sheet you can use for filling in the correct answers on the next page. Or, if you prefer, simply circle the answer numbers in this book. If the book doesn't belong to you, write the numbers 1–35 on a piece of paper and record your answers there. Take as much time as you need to do this short test. When you finish, check your answers against the answer key at the end of this chapter. Each answer tells you which chapter of this book teaches you about the reasoning skill in that question.

1. ⓐ ⓑ ⓒ ⓓ
2. ⓐ ⓑ ⓒ ⓓ
3. ⓐ ⓑ ⓒ ⓓ
4. ⓐ ⓑ ⓒ ⓓ
5. ⓐ ⓑ ⓒ ⓓ
6. ⓐ ⓑ ⓒ ⓓ
7. ⓐ ⓑ ⓒ ⓓ
8. ⓐ ⓑ ⓒ ⓓ
9. ⓐ ⓑ ⓒ ⓓ
10. ⓐ ⓑ ⓒ ⓓ
11. ⓐ ⓑ ⓒ ⓓ
12. ⓐ ⓑ ⓒ ⓓ
13. ⓐ ⓑ ⓒ ⓓ
14. ⓐ ⓑ ⓒ ⓓ
15. ⓐ ⓑ ⓒ ⓓ

16. ⓐ ⓑ ⓒ ⓓ
17. ⓐ ⓑ ⓒ ⓓ
18. ⓐ ⓑ ⓒ ⓓ
19. ⓐ ⓑ ⓒ ⓓ
20. ⓐ ⓑ ⓒ ⓓ
21. ⓐ ⓑ ⓒ ⓓ
22. ⓐ ⓑ ⓒ ⓓ
23. ⓐ ⓑ ⓒ ⓓ
24. ⓐ ⓑ ⓒ ⓓ
25. ⓐ ⓑ ⓒ ⓓ
26. ⓐ ⓑ ⓒ ⓓ
27. ⓐ ⓑ ⓒ ⓓ
28. ⓐ ⓑ ⓒ ⓓ
29. ⓐ ⓑ ⓒ ⓓ
30. ⓐ ⓑ ⓒ ⓓ

31. ⓐ ⓑ ⓒ ⓓ
32. ⓐ ⓑ ⓒ ⓓ
33. ⓐ ⓑ ⓒ ⓓ
34. ⓐ ⓑ ⓒ ⓓ
35. ⓐ ⓑ ⓒ ⓓ

PRETEST

Read the following passage and then answer the questions that follow.

Wendy is a junior in high school and is getting ready to choose a college. She is a serious student and wants to go to the school with the best pre-med program. However, she doesn't want to be too far from home because she wants to visit her sister, who has recently been in a serious accident, on a regular basis. Wendy is likely to obtain scholarships—perhaps even a full scholarship—but she is worried that her parents may not be able to afford whatever costs the scholarships don't cover.

1. Which of the following most accurately presents the issues Wendy must consider, in order of priority?
   a. academic reputation, financial aid, social life on campus
   b. location, financial aid, and academic reputation
   c. financial aid, student services, location
   d. academic reputation, campus environment, and location

2. Which of the following is probably the best choice for Wendy?
   a. The community college, which offers Wendy a full scholarship and has a new but unranked pre-med track.
   b. An expensive liberal arts college, ranked in the top 10 for its pre-med program, which offers Wendy a three-quarters scholarship. The college is a ten-hour drive from Wendy's home.
   c. The state university, ranked in the top 20 for its pre-med program, which offers Wendy a full scholarship for her first two years and guarantees continued scholarships if she maintains at least a B+ grade point average. The state university is two hours away from Wendy's home.
   d. Put off school for a few years until Wendy can save up some money and her sister has recovered. This way, Wendy will be less limited in which school she can choose.

Choose the best answer for each of the following.

3. "There are 52 weeks in a year" is
   a. a fact
   b. an opinion
   c. probably a fact, but I'd have to verify it first
   d. none of the above

4. "Ohio has 22 state forests" is
   a. a fact
   b. an opinion
   c. probably a fact, but I'd have to verify it first
   d. none of the above

5. "There's nothing better than a pepperoni pizza!" is
   a. a fact
   b. an opinion
   c. probably a fact, but I'd have to verify it first
   d. none of the above

What, if anything, is wrong with the following passages?

6. "You don't mean you'd actually support that liar if he ran for re-election, do you?"
   a. The question is unclear and confusing.
   b. The question is unfairly biased against the politician.
   c. The question assumes the listener is going to vote.
   d. There's nothing wrong with the question.

7. "New GingerSnap Soda costs less!"
   a. The ad doesn't tell how much the soda costs.
   b. The ad doesn't tell how much other sodas cost.
   c. The ad doesn't tell what the soda costs less than.
   d. There's nothing wrong with this ad.

8. "Come on, Janet. You're much too smart to pass up this opportunity! Besides, I know what a good and generous person you are."
   a. The speaker is flattering Janet.
   b. The speaker is pressuring Janet.
   c. The speaker is trying to scare Janet.
   d. There's nothing wrong with this passage.

9. "Either we put 40 students in each class or we hire two dozen new teachers. There's no other choice."
   a. The speaker is proposing two equally bad solutions.
   b. The speaker is trying to change the subject.
   c. The speaker isn't allowing for other possibilities, like staggering classes.
   d. There's nothing wrong with this passage.

10. "I wouldn't listen to what Charlie says about anything, and *especially* not what he says about politics. I mean, all he does is watch 'Happy Days' reruns all day. What does he know?"
   a. The speaker assumes that Charlie can't have a valid opinion about politics because he watches "Happy Days" reruns.
   b. The speaker assumes that the listener is stupid enough to listen to Charlie in the first place.
   c. The speaker doesn't like "Happy Days" reruns.
   d. There's nothing wrong with this passage.

11. "I don't think this is right, Zack, because it seems wrong."
   a. The speaker doesn't give Zack a chance to respond.
   b. The reason the speaker offers Zack is the same as the problem the speaker presents.
   c. The problem the speaker presents is too vague.
   d. There's nothing wrong with this passage.

12. "You agree with me, don't you, Marlene? But if you don't, don't worry. The last person who disagreed with me only got fired."
   a. The speaker is using humor inappropriately.
   b. The speaker is trying to get Marlene fired.
   c. The speaker is trying to scare Marlene into agreeing with him.
   d. There's nothing wrong with this passage.

13. "The dishwasher isn't working because it's broken."
   a. The explanation goes in a circle.
   b. The explanation is untestable.
   c. The explanation is irrelevant.
   d. There's nothing wrong with this explanation.

14. "I took two classes and both teachers were terrible. Great—I guess every teacher at this university is lousy."
   a. The speaker doesn't know what makes a good teacher.
   b. The speaker draws an unfair conclusion about all the teachers based on just two classes.
   c. The speaker probably didn't do well in those two classes and is just angry at his teachers.
   d. There's nothing wrong with this passage.

15. "I got straight A's in science in high school, so I should get straight A's in science in college, too."
   a. The speaker is jumping to conclusions.
   b. The speaker is bragging.
   c. The speaker is appealing to our sense of pity.
   d. There's nothing wrong with this passage.

16. "Let's not go out tonight, Abe. I'm really tired, we're trying to save money, and we have to get up early and work tomorrow. A relaxing night at home makes more sense."
   a. The speaker is trying to blame Abe for their problems.
   b. The speaker is trying to make Abe feel sorry for her.
   c. The speaker is biased.
   d. There's nothing wrong with this passage.

17. "If we let Roger stay out until midnight, next thing you know he'll be coming in at 1, then 3, and then not at all."
   a. The speaker is assuming that Roger wants to stay out all night.
   b. The speaker is assuming that X will automatically lead to Y.
   c. The speaker is assuming that X and Y are unacceptable alternatives.
   d. There's nothing wrong with this passage.

18. "I didn't cheat on my taxes. I just used creative accounting techniques."
   a. The speaker is breaking the law.
   b. The speaker is setting a bad example for others.
   c. The speaker is using a slanted phrase for "cheating."
   d. There's nothing wrong with this passage.

19. "I know I didn't do a great job on my paper, Professor Lang. But look at how many students cheated on the exam!"
   a. The student is bringing in an irrelevant issue.
   b. The student is blaming other students for her problems.
   c. The student is making a circular argument.
   d. There's nothing wrong with this passage.

20. "Hey, Todd, check this out! Two weeks ago, I bought this good luck charm, and I've been carrying it around with me every day. Since then, I found $20 in the street, I got the apartment I was hoping for, *and* I got a date with Cindy! This good luck charm really works!"
   a. The speaker believes in good luck charms.
   b. The speaker is assuming that the good luck charm is responsible for his string of good luck.
   c. The speaker doesn't provide enough evidence that the charm works.
   d. There's nothing wrong with this passage.

In the following situations, which source is most credible?

21. Regarding the authenticity of a Van Gogh painting
   a. a professor of art history
   b. a Van Gogh biographer
   c. a contemporary artist
   d. a Van Gogh scholar

22. In defense of a boy accused of stealing from a classmate
   a. his mother
   b. the principal
   c. his teacher
   d. his best friend

Read the following argument carefully and answer the questions that follow.

(1) Censorship of any kind goes against one of our central beliefs as Americans. (2) Nevertheless, certain materials simply should not be accessible on the Internet. (3) The Internet provides users with unlimited access to all kinds of information, but much of that information is inappropriate for immature viewers. (4) Children as young as four or five years old know how to log on and can find sites that feature naked men, women, and even children in provocative poses and engaged in sexual acts. (5) My own 12-year-old son accidentally found a site displaying color photos that would make even Hugh Heffner blush. (6) Worse, some sites allow children to correspond with other site visitors, and the FBI reports that this has led to the kidnapping and even murder of several children across the country.

23. What is the main point (conclusion) of the argument?

  a. sentence 1
  b. sentence 2
  c. sentence 3
  d. sentence 4
  e. sentence 6

24. Which of the following is the strongest support for the conclusion?

  a. sentence 2
  b. sentence 4
  c. sentence 5
  d. sentence 6

25. Sentence 1 does which of the following for the argument?

  a. It weakens the argument by stating that censorship is wrong.
  b. It strengthens the argument by acknowledging the opposition.
  c. It introduces readers to the topic.
  d. It misleads readers by suggesting the argument will be about censorship in general.

Read the following passages carefully and answer the questions that follow.

Roberta lost 10 pounds in February. That month, she put in a great deal of overtime at work. She had also been trying to save money to take a few courses at the community college in the summer. In addition, she had been getting off the bus a mile away from work so that she'd get exercise each day.

26. Which of the following is most likely the *primary cause* of Roberta's weight loss?

  a. She was under too much stress from working so much.
  b. She forgot to eat because she was working so much.
  c. She was trying to save money by not spending it on food.
  d. She was getting exercise each day going to and from work.

27. Using the answer choices in question 26, which of the following can we say with a high degree of confidence?

  a. Both **a** and **d** contributed to her weight loss.
  b. Both **b** and **c** contributed to her weight loss.
  c. Choices **a, b,** and **d** contributed to her weight loss.
  d. All of the above contributed to her weight loss.

28. A young man is walking down the street when he sees that a pile of burning leaves has gotten out of control and the fire is about to spread to the adjacent house. Which of the following should he do first?

  a. Run down the street looking for a phone.
  b. Attempt to put out the fire.
  c. Warn the inhabitants of the house.
  d. Move a safe distance away from the fire.

Ellen is in charge of the annual holiday party for ABC Company. She wants everyone to be happy with the location, so she decides to take a survey. There are 80 employees; 20 are in management, 40 are sales representatives, and 20 are support staff.

29. If Ellen surveys 10 employees, her survey results are
   a. *very likely* to accurately reflect the sentiments of all of the employees.
   b. *likely* to accurately reflect the sentiments of all of the employees.
   c. *very unlikely* to accurately reflect the sentiments of all of the employees.

30. If Ellen surveys 20 employees, who are all members of management, her survey results are
   a. *very likely* to accurately reflect the sentiments of all of the employees.
   b. *likely* to accurately reflect the sentiments of all of the employees.
   c. *very unlikely* to accurately reflect the sentiments of all of the employees.

31. Ellen would get the most accurate results by surveying
   a. 10 managers, 20 salespeople, and 5 support staff
   b. 10 managers, 20 salespeople, and 10 support staff
   c. 20 managers, 20 salespeople, and 20 support staff
   d. 10 managers, 10 salespeople, and 10 support staff

32. Every time you play your stereo loudly, you notice that your upstairs neighbor puts on her stereo loudly, too. When you turn yours down, she turns hers back down. You therefore conclude
   a. your neighbor doesn't like the music you play
   b. your neighbor likes to play her music loudly, too
   c. your neighbor is just showing off her stereo system
   d. your neighbor has to turn up her stereo to drown out yours

33. Beverly is putting together the schedule for her new employees. Each employee has to work 2 days a week. Andrew (A) can only work on Mondays, Wednesdays, and Fridays. Brenda (B) can only work on Mondays, Tuesdays, and Wednesdays. Carla (C) can only work on Tuesdays and Fridays. David (D) can work any day except Wednesday, and Edward (E) can only work on Thursday and Friday. Which of the following is the best schedule?

	Monday	Tuesday	Wednesday	Thursday	Friday
a.	B & D	A & D	A & B	C & E	C & E
b.	A & D	B & C	A & B	D & E	C & E
c.	B & C	C & D	A & D	B & E	A & E
d.	A & D	B & C	C & E	B & E	A & D

Joe, Karl, Larry, and Mike all work for the same company. Joe has been there two years longer than Karl and one year less than Larry. Mike has been there one year longer than Karl. Larry has been there for ten years.

34. Who has been there the longest?
a. Joe
b. Karl
c. Larry
d. Mike

35. Who is the newest employee?
a. Joe
b. Karl
c. Larry
d. Mike

ANSWER KEY

If you miss any of the answers, you can find help for that kind of question in the lesson shown to the right of the answer.

1. b. Lesson 2
2. c. Lesson 2
3. a. Lesson 3
4. c. Lesson 3
5. b. Lesson 3
6. b. Lesson 5
7. c. Lesson 7
8. a. Lesson 11
9. c. Lesson 12
10. a. Lesson 13
11. b. Lesson 12
12. c. Lesson 11
13. a. Lesson 14
14. b. Lesson 16
15. a. Lesson 16
16. d. Lessons 5–9
17. b. Lesson 12
18. c. Lesson 5

19. a. Lesson 13
20. b. Lesson 17
21. d. Lesson 4
22. c. Lesson 4
23. b. Lesson 6
24. d. Lessons 8, 9
25. b. Lesson 9
26. d. Lesson 17
27. a. Lesson 17
28. c. Lessons 2, 20
29. c. Lesson 18
30. c. Lesson 18
31. b. Lesson 18
32. d. Lesson 15
33. b. Lesson 20
34. c. Lessons 15, 20
35. b. Lessons 15, 20

CRITICAL THINKING AND LOGIC SKILLS LESSONS 1–20

L·E·S·S·O·N
CRITICAL THINKING AND REASONING SKILLS

1

LESSON SUMMARY

As a college student, you will be expected to master a great deal of information in the form of facts, ideas, terms, and techniques. While it's important to be able to remember that information, your success—both in college and beyond—rests on your ability to think critically and logically *about* that information. Critical thinking and reasoning skills may, in fact, be the most important skills can you develop during your college career.

No matter who you are or what you do, you have to make decisions. You may not realize it, but even those decisions that seem like second nature—like deciding what to wear when you're getting dressed in the morning—require some critical thinking and reasoning skills. When you decide what to wear, you take many factors into consideration—the weather forecast; the current temperature; your plans for the day (where are you going? who will you see?); your comfort level (will you be walking a lot? sitting all day?); and so on. Thus you are already a critical thinker on some level. But your life is complicated, and you face decisions that are much more difficult than choosing what to wear. How do you handle a conflict? Solve a problem? Resolve a crisis? Make a moral or ethical decision?

> "The person who thinks before he acts seldom has to apologize for his acts."
>
> —Napoleon Hill
> (Author, *Think and Grow Rich*)

While there's no guarantee you'll always make the right decision or find the most effective solution to a problem, there *is* a way to significantly improve your odds—and that is by improving your critical thinking and reasoning skills.

WHAT ARE CRITICAL THINKING AND REASONING SKILLS?

To improve your critical thinking and reasoning skills, you need to know exactly what they are.

CRITICAL THINKING SKILLS

Think for a minute about the words *critical thinking*. What does this phrase mean? Essentially, **critical thinking** is a decision-making process. Specifically, critical thinking means carefully considering a problem, claim, question, or situation in order to determine the best solution. That is, when you think critically, you take the time to consider all sides of an issue, evaluate evidence, and imagine different scenarios and possible outcomes. It sounds like a lot of work, but the same basic critical thinking skills can be applied to all types of situations.

Critical thinking is so important because it helps you determine:

- How to best solve a problem
- Whether to accept or reject a claim

- How to best answer a question
- How to best handle a situation

REASONING SKILLS

Where critical thinking skills help you determine *how* to get from point A, the problem, to point B, the solution, reasoning skills help ensure that your solution makes good, logical sense. That is, you can get from A to B haphazardly, or you can get there by reason.

A **reason** is a motive or cause for something—a justification for thoughts, actions, opinions, and so on. In other words, it's *why* you do, say, or think what you do. But your reasons for doing things aren't always reasonable—as you know if you've ever done or said something in anger. In other words, **reasoning skills** ask you to use good sense and base your reasons for doing things in facts, evidence, or logical conclusions rather than just on your emotions. When you decide on the best way to handle a situation or determine the best solution to a problem, you should have good *logical* (rather than purely *emotional)* reasons for coming to that conclusion.

Critical Thinking Skills: Carefully considering a problem, claim, question, or situation to determine the best solution
- Consider all sides of an issue
- Carefully evaluate evidence
- Imagine different possible scenarios and outcomes

Reasoning Skills: Using facts, evidence, logical conclusions, and good common sense to justify a decision or course of action
- Distinguish between logic and emotion
- Conclusions based on evidence
- Conclusions based on good common sense

To clarify the difference between critical thinking and reasoning skills, imagine the following situation:

> It's Tuesday. You have an essay due tomorrow at noon, and you haven't started it yet. It's 2:00 in the afternoon, and you're scheduled to work from 5:00 to 10:00 in the Media Center.

Using Critical Thinking Skills

What do you do? First, apply your critical thinking skills and consider all of your options. You could:

- Get someone to cover your shift at work
- Call in sick
- Just not show up for work
- Just not do the paper
- Stay up all night and get the paper done
- Ask the professor for an extension
- Not talk to the professor and just hand the paper in late

Next, consider the evidence or the facts of the case. You know:

- You usually write well when you're under pressure
- You have a good idea of what you want to write about
- Your professor has given other students extensions in the past
- You've already called in sick three times in the last month
- You really need the money
- Tuesday nights are usually very slow at the Media Center
- The only person who could cover for you at work is Stacey, and she's in your class, so she'll probably also be working on her essay

- You've never been late for class and you've handed in all of your assignments on time.
- You're doing well in the class so far and get along well with the professor.
- Your professor may not accept your essay if it's late and you don't ask for an extension.
- The essay is worth 20% of your grade for this class

Now, imagine possible scenarios and outcomes:

- You may not get in touch with your professor
- You may get in touch with your professor and she may say no to an extension
- You may lose your job if you call in sick again
- Stacey may have already finished her paper and be willing to cover for you
- You may be very busy at work
- You may have some kind of emergency that would keep you from getting your paper done tonight
- You may fall asleep while working

Using Reasoning Skills

Now that you've carefully considered the situation, you're ready to make a decision. Your reasoning skills now come into play as you choose among your options. You might, for example, decide to go to work and try to finish your paper by noon tomorrow. Here's why:

- You want to keep a clean track record with your professor—no late papers
- You've been thinking about the paper for some time. You have a thesis and a rough outline in your head
- You have three hours before work that you can devote to drafting your essay

- The Media Center will probably be very slow, so it's likely you'll have a few hours to work on your essay at work
- You can work on your essay from 10:00 until noon tomorrow, if you have to
- You write well under pressure
- You need the money, so you don't want to give up the hours at work
- You need to keep your job

> **Logical**: according to reason; according to conclusions drawn from evidence or good common sense
>
> **Emotional**: drawn from emotions, from intense mental feelings

THE DIFFERENCE BETWEEN REASON AND EMOTION

In the preceding example, the reasons given for tackling the essay assignment are good, logical reasons, not ones based on emotion. But it would be false to say that anything emotional is not reasonable. In fact, it's perfectly valid to take your emotions into consideration when you make decisions. After all, how you feel is very important. But if there's *no* logic or reason behind your decisions or if your emotions are so powerful that you ignore good common sense, you're usually in for trouble.

Let's say, for example, that you're embarrassed about having procrastinated on your essay, and you're ashamed to ask for an extension. Thus you decide to try to finish your paper on time. Now you might end up getting your paper done by noon, but you can see that there's a big difference in the reasoning skills at work

here and in the earlier example. Before, you had a series of good, logical reasons for not asking for the extension; here, your decision is based purely on your pride. You might end up with the same result in both cases, but decisions based on emotions rather than logic are often problematic. For example, say the situation were slightly different: You don't have a thesis and outline in your head, you don't have much free time at work, and you don't have several hours to write in the morning. If you decide not to ask for an extension because you're too embarrassed, you risk not getting your paper done on time and losing 20% of your grade as a result.

Consider another example. Let's say that you got an internship with a company off campus and you need to buy a car. Choosing which car to buy is a rather big decision, so it's important that you make it wisely. You'll want to be sure you use your critical thinking and reasoning skills to:

- Carefully consider your options
- Consider different possibilities and scenarios
- Have logical reasons to support your final decision

It may seem obvious that you need to choose a car that best suits your lifestyle and budget. As much as you might like sports cars, as much fun as they may be to drive, you shouldn't buy the new Special Edition Corvette if you have to pay your own tuition. But for a variety of emotional reasons, many people *do* make these kinds of unwise and un-reasonable decisions. They may have thought about the situation critically and still made the wrong choice because they let their emotions override their sense of logic and reason. Similarly, others often try to influence our decisions by appealing to our emotions instead of our sense of reason. We'll discuss some common appeals to emotion in Lesson 11.

PRACTICE

1. For practice, consider how you applied your critical thinking and reasoning skills to a decision you recently made: How you decided to attend this college or university. What different things did you take into consideration when you were thinking about which college or university to attend? List at least five different considerations below. One issue is listed to get you started. (You'll find a full sample list at the end of this lesson.)

Things to consider:

- Tuition
-
-
-
-

Share your list with others in your class. Are there any issues that you didn't consider that someone else did? Did you overlook any issues that you think you should have considered in your decision-making process?

JUSTIFYING YOUR DECISION

One way to help ensure that you're using your critical thinking and reasoning skills is to always *justify* your decisions and actions. *Why* did you do what you did? Why did you make that decision? Why did that seem like the best solution? Try justifying even your most everyday decisions and actions, like what you chose to eat for lunch or where you decide to sit in class. You'll get to know your current decision-making process, and you'll be able to determine where in that process you can be more effective.

You may find, for example, that you make certain decisions based on what you want others to think of you rather than on what you really want to do. Or you may find that you go to the other extreme—that you ignore your own emotions completely when making decisions. By looking honestly at why you do what you do, you'll see where you use logical reasoning skills and when you make decisions haphazardly or based solely on your emotions.

PRACTICE

2. Evaluate your reasons for choosing the college or university you attend. First, list your reasons. Then, look over your list carefully. Put an asterisk (*) next to those reasons you think are logical and a dash (—) next to those reasons you think are emotional. While it's certainly valid to have several dashes on your list, the bulk of the items should have an asterisk next to them. (You'll find a sample list at the end of this lesson.)

WHY CRITICAL THINKING AND REASONING SKILLS ARE IMPORTANT

Whatever your role in life—student, employee, friend, parent—you will face situations that will require you to use critical thinking and reasoning skills. By improving these skills, you can improve your success in literally everything you do. Specifically, strong critical thinking and reasoning skills will help you:

- Compose and support strong, logical arguments
- Assess the validity of other people's arguments
- Make more effective and logical decisions
- Solve problems and puzzles more efficiently and effectively

In a sense, all of these four skills are involved in what can be called *problem solving situations*. If someone wants to change your mind and convince you of something, you have a "problem"—you have to decide whether or not to change your beliefs, whether to accept that person's argument. Similarly, when you have a choice to make, or a position you'd like to support, you have a different type of "problem" to solve— what choice to make, how to support your position. Thus, this book will use the term *problem solving* to refer to any one of these situations. Problem solving will be the focus of the next lesson.

PRACTICE

Use your critical thinking and reasoning skills to solve the following problem. Sample answers are given at the end of this lesson.

Jorge, an accounting major, is about to graduate. He's been offered two jobs. One offer is from United Casualty, where he worked for the last two summers as an intern. The other is from United Casualty's main competitor, The Harrison Group. Harrison is willing to pay Jorge a little more for a comparable position, but Jorge really likes the people at United. What should Jorge do?

3. List the different issues Jorge should consider in making this difficult decision.

4. Make a decision for Jorge and explain why that's a good decision for him. Feel free to make up the various circumstances in his life—for example, that Jorge lives close to United but would have to relocate to work for Harrison (but he's always wanted to live on the West Coast). The details are up to you; what matters is that you successfully justify his decision. The more reasons you can give for his decision—and the more logical they are—the better.

IN SHORT

Critical thinking is the act of carefully considering a problem, claim, question, or situation in order to determine the best "solution." Reasoning skills, which go hand-in-hand with critical thinking, ask you to base your decisions in facts, evidence, or logical conclusions. Critical thinking and reasoning skills work together to help you make smarter decisions and solve problems effectively. They also help you make stronger arguments and better evaluate the arguments of others.

Skill Building Until Next Time

Notice how many decisions you make throughout the day and how many different problems you face. What kind of decisions and problems do you encounter most often at home? At work? At school?
- Write down the process you went through to make a decision or solve a problem today. What did you do to get from point A, the problem, to point B, the solution?
- Evaluate a decision or problem you solved recently. Do you think it was a wise decision or effective solution? Why or why not? Did you consider the range of issues, or did you neglect to take certain issues into consideration? Did you make your decision based mostly on reason or mostly on your emotions?

ANSWERS

1. You probably listed several important issues like these:

- Location of campus
- Degree programs available
- Financial aid
- Size of student body
- Reputation
- Student/faculty ratio
- Student life (activities, sports, clubs)
- Job placement rate
- Faculty members
- Academic standards and rigor
- Diversity of student body
- Campus environment
- Housing

2. Actual lists will vary. Here's one possibility:

- Close to home—don't have to pay for housing*
- Campus is beautiful–
- Library has impressive collection of books and electronic resources*
- Several state-of-the-art computer labs*
- One of the best colleges in the state for my major*
- State school—tuition reduction*
- Exciting campus night life–
- Student body is small—won't feel lost in the crowd–
- Student body is small—more attention from instructors*
- Terrific study-abroad program*

3. Some of the issues Jorge needs to consider include:

- Money
- Job security
- Benefits
- Compatibility with coworkers
- Job environment
- Specific job duties
- Location/commute
- Hours
- Room for advancement
- Stability of company

4. Answers will vary. Here's one possibility:

Jorge should take the job with Harrison. Though he really likes the people he's worked with at United, there is limited room for advancement. At Harrison, Jorge will automatically be placed on the management track. Harrison will also pay Jorge more money, which is important since he has several large student loans. Harrison is a stable company—it's been in business for over 40 years and had a record year last year. United, on the other hand, is only 10 years old and has recently had a great deal of employee turnover. Furthermore, Jorge has always wanted to live on the West Coast. Harrison will pay for Jorge's relocation costs and help him find an apartment.

L · E · S · S · O · N
PROBLEM SOLVING STRATEGIES

LESSON SUMMARY

You face problems every day, and sometimes they can seem overwhelming. In this lesson, you'll learn how to make a problem more manageable by pinpointing the main issue and breaking it down into its various parts.

H ouston, we have a problem." This famous line, captured in the hit movie *Apollo 13*, turns out to be quite an understatement—the astronauts and ground crew of Apollo 13 faced a number of very serious problems. In one of the movie's most memorable scenes, a team of engineers must literally make a square peg fit into a round hole—and fast. The lives of the astronauts depend on it.

Fortunately, not all problems are life-and-death situations. But everyone faces his or her share of problems, and it's important to handle problems quickly and effectively. Critical thinking and reasoning skills can help you do just that.

DEFINITION: WHAT'S A PROBLEM?

Let's begin by defining the word *problem*. In terms of critical thinking and reasoning skills, a **problem** is any situation where you must make a difficult decision. That decision can be anything—how to answer a difficult question, how to handle a difficult situation, how to convince someone to see your point of view, or even how to solve a puzzle or mystery. For example, you might face the following kinds of problems:

Questions: Should abortion be legal?

Should you report your colleague for stealing?

Situations: Your friends are pressing you to go to a party tonight, but you promised your roommate you'd help him on a project. What do you do?

Your client has offered you a small bribe to keep an indiscretion private. How should you handle the situation?

Convincing: How do you convince Joe that he shouldn't treat his girlfriend that way?

How can you convince your boss you deserve a raise?

Solving: Who stole the money from the safe?

How can you fit in a double major and still graduate on time?

> **Problem:** any situation where a difficult decision must be made

IDENTIFYING THE PROBLEM

The first step to solving any problem is to *identify* the problem. This may sound obvious—of course you need to know what the problem is. But it's important to take this step, because in real life, with all its complications, it's easy to lose sight of the real problem at hand. When this happens, the problem becomes much

more complicated than it need be because you end up focusing on secondary issues rather than what's really at stake.

Identifying the problem is much like identifying the thesis of an essay. You might ask of the essay, "What is the author's main point? What is the overall idea he or she is trying to prove?" Similarly, when faced with a problem, you should ask: "What is the main issue? What is the key question that needs to be answered or situation that needs to be resolved? If I step back and look at the 'big picture,' what is it that needs to happen?"

Once you've identified the problem, you need to break it down into its parts. This is an essential step because it gives you a sense of the **scope** of the problem. How big is it? How many issues are there? Sometimes, at first glance, problems seem so big that a solution seems impossible. Other times, you may underestimate the size of a problem and end up making a poor decision because you've overlooked an important factor. By breaking a problem down into its parts, you may find it's not as big a problem as you thought—or that it's much more complicated than you initially anticipated. Either way, when you break a problem down, you make it manageable. Big or small, you can take it one issue at a time.

PRACTICE

To see exactly how breaking down a problem works, look at a sample scenario. You'll find the answer at the end of this lesson.

Your car has broken down and will have to be in the shop for two or three days. It's Monday, and you need to get to work, which is 20 miles north of where you live. The nearest bus stop is 10 miles away to the east. Your brother, who lives near you, works 20 miles to the south. The nearest cab company is 20 miles to the west.

1. Which of the following best expresses the real issue or problem?
   a. how you will be able to afford the repairs
   b. how you can convince your brother to give you a ride
   c. how you are going to get to work
   d. whether you will be able to afford a cab

Try another scenario. This one is a bit more complicated than the first. To get the best answer, you need to ask yourself where the real issue lies, what's really at stake. Is it more important to determine what happened, or to decide how to fix what happened?

You manage a small graphic design group. You've delegated an important project for a local charity to a group of three designers who don't have the design prototypes ready when they're due. There also seems to be a great deal of tension among the team members.

2. Which of the following best expresses the real issue or problem?
   a. why the designs aren't ready
   b. what to tell the client
   c. who is to blame
   d. why the team members aren't getting along
   e. how to get the designs done as quickly as possible
   f. how to prevent your team from missing future deadlines

BREAKING THE PROBLEM INTO ITS PARTS

Successful problem solving, like most skills, requires a certain strategic approach. You'll get the best results when you are clear about your goal (the main problem to be solved) and when you follow a logical order of doing things. Thus, once you identify the main problem, you need to break the problem down into its various parts (issues) so that you can address the various things that need to be done. The next step is to prioritize those issues so that you have a "recipe" of sorts to guide you.

Breaking a problem down into its parts means exactly that. You know the main issue, the big picture; now, what are all the pieces of this problem? What separate issues have to be dealt with in order to deal with that big picture? For example, here are some of the parts of the design problem:

- What caused the delay
- What to tell the client
- Who is to blame

Each of these issues comes with issues of its own to address. For example, let's say the team didn't finish the project on time because the designers were unable to agree upon a design. This raises several other issues:

- Whether they understand what exactly it is that the client wants
- Whether their lack of agreement stems from personal or professional differences
- Whether they understand the importance of meeting deadlines
- Whether you were effective in managing the team

Remember that our definition of **problem** includes more than just difficult situations like the one described in question 2. Questions, attempts to convince or persuade, puzzles, and all kinds of conflicts can be broken down in this manner. In fact, you can use this problem-solving approach to tackle various assignments and make better arguments. For example, imagine you receive the following assignment:

Write a three- to five-page essay on a controversial topic, such as the death penalty. Your essay should aim to convince readers of the validity of your point of view.

You've decided to write about free needle exchange programs, and you've identified your main problem as the following:

Problem: How can I convince readers that free needle exchange programs make good sense?

Now, you can use your critical thinking and reasoning skills to list the parts of the problem:

- Who are my readers?
- What do my readers know about needle exchange programs?
- What evidence is there that needle exchange programs are a benefit to society?
- Are there studies, samples, statistics to cite?
- What arguments do people make against needle exchange programs?
- How can I introduce the topic to make readers sympathetic to my thesis?
- What does it cost to run needle exchange programs? Who pays?
- How would society benefit from free needle exchange programs?

- How is society suffering without free needle exchange programs?

By approaching your essay assignment as a critical thinking problem, you can make your writing task more manageable and your final product more effective.

PRACTICE

3. Imagine that the design team from the scenario in question 2 didn't finish the project on time because they were unable to agree upon a design. Imagine also that the lack of agreement among the designers stems from personal differences. What additional problems do you now need to consider? List them below. One is listed to get you started. (You'll find a sample answer at the end of this lesson.)
   - How can you find out what those differences are?
   -
   -
   -
   -

PRIORITIZING ISSUES

Once you've identified the parts of the problem, the next step is to decide how to tackle those issues. Clearly, some issues are more important than others, and some must be addressed before others. That's why it's essential to rank the parts of the problem in the order in which you think they should be addressed. Which issues need to be dealt with first? Second? Third? Are there some issues that must be solved before you can deal with others?

Imagine, for example, that you simply commanded your design team to finish the project in one hour, without first considering *why* it wasn't already done. If it wasn't done because no one on the team knew what the client wanted, the job probably still wouldn't get done. Until the root of the problem is found, progress may be at an impasse.

Because every problem is different, there are no hard and fast rules about how to prioritize them. Ranking issues in the order in which they should be addressed is largely a matter of common sense. Once you've listed the parts of the problem, look carefully at that list. If you were to tackle each issue, in what order would you do it? Remember that certain things cannot happen unless other things happen first. Remember also that certain solutions will be more effective if other actions have already taken place. You can think of prioritizing the issues as connecting the dots: Tackling the issues in a certain order will give you the big picture; addressing the issues randomly might result in a meaningless scribble.

PRACTICE

4. Use your critical thinking and reasoning skills to list the parts of the following problem (one is already given). Then, prioritize those issues. A sample answer is given at the end of this lesson.

Situation: A colleague is lying to prospective clients in order to get business.
Problem: What should you do about it?
Parts of the problem:
- Why is he lying?
-
-
-
-

-
-

Order in which the parts should be addressed:
1.
2.
3.
4.
5.

RELEVANCE OF ISSUES

When you're breaking down a problem, it's important that you make sure that each issue is *relevant* to the problem. That is, each issue should be clearly related to the matter at hand. It's often obvious when something *isn't* relevant. Whether you like your pizza plain or with pepperoni, for example, clearly has nothing to do with whether or not you should report your colleague. But an issue like whether he might try to exact some sort of revenge on you if you report him might be relevant. It depends upon your relationship and what kind of person he is. Similarly, if you are trying to convince readers that needle exchange programs are beneficial to society, you'll need to consider the relevance of issues. Does it matter where the money to fund such these programs comes from? Certainly. Does it matter whether similar programs have worked in other countries? Probably, though it depends upon just how comparable the social, economic, and political situations are in those other countries. Does it matter that there's a new drug to treat people infected with HIV? Probably not, since needle exchange programs are about *preventing* the spread of HIV in the first place, not what to do once it's contracted.

One thing to keep in mind is that personal preferences are often brought in as issues when they shouldn't be. For example, you may like one person on your design team more than the others, but that doesn't automatically mean that that person is more believable or less responsible for the problem than the others. In other words, your friendship with one or the other, or lack thereof, should not be relevant to the situation. Lesson 4 has more to say about this kind of bias.

PRACTICE

Read the following scenario carefully and then answer the questions that follow. Sample answers are given at the end of this lesson.

You just inherited a large amount of money from your great uncle. In his will, however, he specified that you must invest that money for ten years before you can withdraw any cash. Your spouse says you should invest in the stock market. Your father says the stock market is too risky, that you should put the money right in the bank. Your friend says put the money in mutual funds—they're less risky than the market but give you a better return than the bank.

5. The main problem or issue is
    a. whether or not stocks are too risky
    b. whether putting the money in the bank gives high enough return
    c. whose advice you should take
    d. how you should invest the money

6. What are the parts of the problem?

7. In what order should you address the parts of the problem?

IN SHORT

Problems are any situation where you must make a difficult decision. Effective problem solving, of course, depends upon good critical thinking and reasoning skills. Once you identify the problem, you need to consider all aspects of the problem so you can break it down into its parts. That's a critical thinking skill. When you prioritize the issues, you use your reasoning skills to place the parts of the problem in logical order. Likewise, determining whether or not issues are relevant is a matter of good common sense and your ability to see whether or not there are logical connections between issues.

Skill Building Until Next Time

- Take a problem that you come across today and break it down. Identify the main issue and each of its parts. Then, prioritize the parts.
- Observe how someone you see on a regular basis—a roommate, co-worker, sibling—handles a complex problem. Is he or she able to correctly identify the real problem? Does he or she break it down into its parts to make it more manageable? Does he or she prioritize the issues? Evaluate this person's problem-solving strategy.

ANSWERS

1. The answer, of course, is **c**—how you are going to get to work. This is the overall problem you must solve—the "big picture."

Notice how each of the other possible answers above is a *sub*-issue; each option except **c** is a *specific* way to address the larger, more general, (main) problem. It's important to remember that **a, b,** and **d** are just *parts* of the problem, and there are other parts that are not listed here. If one of these options doesn't work out, several other viable options remain.

2. It's very easy to get caught up in who is to blame for the missed deadline. Did one of the designers not do his or her share of work? Are you to blame for not checking on the group's progress? While these are indeed important questions, the real problem is to figure out how to get the job done as quickly as possible (choice **e**). After all, you have an obligation to your client and a job that you want to keep.

In order to solve this problem, you *do* need to address several of the other issues above. You need to know, for example, why the designs aren't ready before you can move forward. Is it because someone didn't do what he or she was supposed to do? Is it because the design team is missing some crucial information? Is it because the design team was unable to agree upon a design? Similarly, you'll need to address the issue of what to tell the client, who is expecting the work to be completed. And you'll definitely need to get the team working together smoothly in order to complete the project quickly. Of course, once this problem is solved, you'll want to consider **f**, how to prevent your team from missing another deadline.

3. You might have added the following issues:
- How can you get team members to communicate their difficulties to you?
- How can you help resolve those differences?
- Have any of the team members acted inappropriately?
- How should you exercise your authority?
- How can you change your management techniques to be more aware of problems like this in the future?

4. Answers will vary. Here are some possible issues prioritized:

1. Why is he lying?
2. What kind of lies is he telling? How serious are they?
3. What will happen when the clients discover the company can't provide what he's promised?
4. Do you have evidence of your colleague's improper behavior?
5. What will happen to your colleague if you report him?
6. What will happen to your colleague if you don't?
7. What will happen to your company if you don't?
8. What will happen to your relationship with your colleague if you report him? If you don't?
9. Can you live with yourself if you don't report him? If you do?
10. How would you go about reporting him? To whom?

5. The main problem is **d,** how you should invest the money.

6. You may have broken the problem down into the following parts:

- How can I find out about these options?
- What are the different options for investing?
- What does my spouse think?
- What kind of investment gives me the most return?
- What kind of investment gives me the most security?
- What's more important to me—return or security?
- Whose opinion should I trust?

7. You should probably address the parts of the problem in the following order:

1. What's more important to me, return or security?
2. What does my spouse think?
3. What are the different options for investing?
4. How can I find out about these options?
5. Whose opinion should I trust?
6. What kind of investment gives me the most return?
7. What kind of investment gives me the most security?

L·E·S·S·O·N 3
THINKING VS. KNOWING

LESSON SUMMARY

One of the keys to good critical thinking and reasoning skills is the ability to distinguish between fact and opinion. This lesson will show you the difference—and why it matters.

D o you believe in aliens? UFOs? Do you believe that beings from outer space have made contact with Earth? However you answer, you are, of course, expressing an *opinion*.

Whether or not aliens exist is a matter of *fact*. That is, technically, the existence of aliens—and whether or not they've made contact—can be *proven* to be true or false. But until there is enough evidence to prove one way or the other, people have to go on their opinions—what they *believe* to be true.

DEFINITIONS: FACT VS. OPINION

Before we go any further, let's define *fact* and *opinion*.

Facts are:

- Things *known* for certain to have happened
- Things *known* for certain to be true
- Things *known* for certain to exist

Opinions, on the other hand, are:
- Things *believed* to have happened
- Things *believed* to be true
- Things *believed* to exist

Essentially, the difference between fact and opinion is the difference between *believing* and *knowing*. Opinions may be *based* on facts, but they are still what we *think*, not what we *know*. Opinions are debatable; facts usually are not. A good test for whether something is a fact or opinion is to ask yourself, "Can this statement be debated? Is this known for certain to be true?" If you can answer *yes* to the first question, you have an opinion; if you answer *yes* to the second, you have a fact. If you're not sure, then it's best to assume that it's an opinion until you can *verify* that it is indeed a fact.

> **Fact:** not debatable; based on what is **known**
> **Opinion:** debatable; based on what someone **believes**

WHY THE DIFFERENCE BETWEEN FACT AND OPINION IS IMPORTANT

When you're making decisions, it's important to be able to distinguish between fact and opinion—between what you or others *believe* and what you or others *know* to be true. When you make decisions, assess others' arguments, and support your own arguments, facts will generally carry more weight than opinions. For example, if you want to convince your boss that you deserve a raise, and you present him with facts about your performance as an employee, you're much more likely to get that raise than if you simply use the opinion "I think I deserve one." Look at the difference between these two examples:

- "I really think I should get a raise. It's about time, and I deserve it. I've earned it."
- "I really think I deserve a raise. I've met all of my production goals since I've been here, my evaluations have been excellent, and I was employee of the month. . . ."

Notice that the first example merely expresses your opinion. In the second example, however, several facts support the opinion that "I deserve a raise."

Distinguishing between fact and opinion is important for two other reasons:

- People will often present their opinions as fact. When you're trying to make big decisions or solve serious problems, you need to know that you're working with evidence rather than emotions.
- Opinions that are based on facts (like the second argument that you should get a raise) are far more valid than opinions offered with no such support.

PRACTICE

Read the following statements carefully. Which of the following are facts? Opinions? Write an F in the blank if it is a fact and an O if it is an opinion. The answers are given at the end of this lesson.

_____ **1.** People who have been out of school and in the work force for several years make better students.

_____ **2.** More people are working for a few years before they go to college than ever before.

____**3.** Many companies provide tuition reimbursement for adults returning to school for college degrees.

____**4.** Most companies don't provide enough tuition reimbursement for their employees.

____**5.** At Hornig Financial Services, you won't get reimbursed unless you earn at least a C in any course you take.

To strengthen your ability to distinguish between fact and opinion, try responding to a fact with an opinion. Here's a fact:

Americans pay federal, state, and local taxes.

An opinion is something debatable. Here are two opinions in response to the fact above:

Americans pay too much in taxes.

Americans should pay taxes only if they make over $40,000.

Now you try. Sample answers are given at the end of this lesson.

6. Fact: Some states have raised their speed limits to 65 or more on major highways.
Opinion:

7. Fact: Many Native American tribes have asked to be recognized as independent, sovereign nations.
Opinion:

8. Fact: E-mail and other technologies are making it possible for more people to work from home than ever before.
Opinion:

9. Fact: Most college students are required to take some liberal arts *and* science courses, no matter what their majors.
Opinion:

TENTATIVE TRUTHS

The difference between fact and opinion is not always a black-and-white issue. To illustrate this point, label the following as either fact (F) or opinion (0).

____1. I believe Edison, Inc. and A-Best Papers are guilty of price-fixing.
____2. Edison, Inc. and A-Best Papers are guilty of price-fixing.

You didn't by chance mark the first claim as **O** and the second claim as **F,** did you? If you did, it's easy to see why. The phrase "I believe" makes it clear that the first claim is expressing an opinion. The second claim, however, is stated matter-of-factly. But is it true? Can you accept it as a fact just because it sounds like one? Statements like number 2 fall into a category *between* fact and opinion called **tentative truths**. A tentative truth sounds like a fact, but because there's no *evidence* that the claim is true, it can only be accepted as a *possible* truth, pending verification.

> **Fact:** Not debatable; something **known** for certain to have happened, to be true, or to exist
> **Tentative Truth:** Needs verification; something that **may** have happened, be true, or exist
> **Opinion:** Debatable; something **believed** to have happened, to be true, or to exist.

Evidence is one thing that enables us to accept tentative truths as fact. If you were to see good evidence of Edison and A-Best's price-fixing, then you'd certainly be wise to remove statement 2 from the tentative truth category and call it a fact.

DECIDING FACTORS

What about tentative truths that you are unable to verify and that are presented without any evidence? How do you know just how tentative you should be about accepting that claim as true? The answer depends upon two key questions:

1. Does the claim conflict with what you already know to be true—your own personal experience, your background knowledge, generally accepted theories, or good common sense?
2. Does the claim come from a credible source—someone who is trustworthy or who is an authority on the subject?

Imagine that a student in your biology class tells you that amphibians evolved from mammals. Why should you accept this as a very tentative truth at best? Because it conflicts with what you know about evolution, and because it conflicts with common sense.

Now let's imagine that this claim comes from your biology professor and not a fellow student. Even though the claim conflicts with what you already know to be true, you should be more willing to tentatively accept the claim as true. Why? Because of its source. After all, you wouldn't expect your professor to tell you erroneous information, especially in his or her area of expertise.

It is important to note, however, that once in a while, professors *do* make mistakes and they may, on occasion, present opinions as facts. Far more frequently, however, professors express opinions as opinions—but because they're professors, students often accept their opinions as fact. Your professors' education and experience should certainly command your respect, but not your blind acceptance of everything your professors have to say. What most professors want, in fact, is the opposite: for you to be able to think critically about the ideas and opinions they present and come to your own conclusions. (The initial claim, by the way, is, of course, false. Mammals evolved from reptiles, which evolved from amphibians.)

PRACTICE

Determine whether the following claims are facts (F), opinions (O), or claims that you should accept as tentative truths (TT).

_____ **10.** Most citizens of India live below the poverty level.

_____ **11.** Bombay is an intoxicating city.

_____ **12.** India gained independence from Britain in 1947.

FACT VS. OPINION IN CRITICAL REASONING

Now let's look at a situation where you have to use your critical thinking and reasoning skills to make a decision and where it will be important to distinguish between fact and opinion. Let's return to the example where you must invest your inheritance from your great uncle. In order to make a good decision, you need to know the difference between fact and opinion. You also have to be able to recognize when opinions are based on facts. First, let's just continue practicing the distinction between fact and opinion.

PRACTICE

13. Read the following paragraphs carefully. **Highlight** the facts and <u>underline</u> the opinions.

Paragraph A:

There are lots of different ways to invest your money. Many people invest in stocks and bonds, but I think good old-fashioned savings accounts and CDs (certificates of deposit) are the best way to invest your hard-earned money. Stocks and bonds are often risky, and it doesn't make sense to gamble with your hard-earned money. True, regular savings accounts and CDs can't make you a millionaire overnight or provide the high returns some stock investments do. But unless you're an expert, it's hard to know which stocks will provide you with that kind of return. Besides, savings accounts and CDs are fully insured and provide steady, secure interest on your money. That makes a whole lot of cents.

Paragraph B:

Many folks are scared of the stock market—but they shouldn't be. True, the stock market is risky, but the gamble is worth it. Besides, playing it safe requires too much patience. The stock market is by far the best option for today's investors.

14. Now that you've distinguished fact from opinion in these paragraphs, which paragraph should you take more seriously when deciding what to do with your uncle's inheritance? Write your answer on a separate piece of paper. A sample answer is given at the end of this lesson.

IN SHORT

Distinguishing between fact and opinion is a vital critical thinking and reasoning skill. To make wise decisions and solve problems effectively, you need to know the difference between what people *think* (opinion) and what people *know* (fact); between what people *believe* to be true (opinion) and what *has been proven* to be true (fact). You'll also be able to determine whether something presented as fact is really true or if you should accept it as a tentative truth.

Skill Building Until Next Time

- Listen carefully to what people say today and try to determine whether they are stating a fact or expressing an opinion. If you're not sure, is it OK to accept it as a tentative truth?
- As you come across facts and opinions today, practice turning them into their opposites: make facts out of opinions and opinions out of facts.

ANSWERS

1. O
2. F
3. F
4. O
5. F

6. These states are endangering the lives of their citizens.

7. The U.S. government should grant all Native American tribes their sovereignty.

8. E-mail and other technologies are great because they enable us to work from home and spend more time with our families.

9. It's important for students to have some background in both liberal arts and the sciences.

10. **TT.** Even if you know that many people in India live in poverty, you should probably accept this as a tentative truth since the claim is that "most" citizens live below the poverty level. This needs to be verified.

11. O

12. **F.** If you know your world history, you will immediately recognize this as fact. If, however, you don't know much about England's colonization of India, then accept this as a tentative truth until you verify the information.

13. **Paragraph A**

There are lots of different ways to invest your money. Many people invest in stocks and bonds, but I think good old-fashioned savings accounts and CDs (certificates of deposit) are the best way to invest your hard-earned money. **Stocks and bonds are often risky,** and it doesn't make sense to gamble with your hard-earned money. **True, regular savings accounts and CDs can't make you a millionaire overnight or provide the high returns some stock investments do.** But unless you're an expert, it's hard to know which stocks will provide you with that kind of return. Besides, **savings accounts and CDs are fully insured and provide steady, secure interest on your money.** That makes a whole lot of cents.

Paragraph B

Many folks are scared of the stock market—but they shouldn't be. **True, the stock market is risky,** but the gamble is worth it. Besides, playing it safe requires too much patience. The stock market is by far the best option for today's investors.

14. You should have chosen **Paragraph A** as the paragraph to take more seriously. Paragraph A has a good balance of fact and opinion; most of the writer's opinions are supported by facts. Paragraph B, on the other hand, includes several unsupported opinions. Of course, how seriously you take either paragraph depends on who wrote these paragraphs. We'll examine the issue of credibility next.

L·E·S·S·O·N

WHO MAKES THE CLAIM?

4

LESSON SUMMARY

When we're faced with opinions and tentative truths, it's important to know how much we can trust our sources and how much they know about the subject at hand. This lesson will teach you how to evaluate credibility so that you can better judge your sources and therefore make better decisions.

You've decided you'd like to see a movie tonight, but you're not sure what to see. You're thinking about catching the latest Steven Spielberg film, so you decide to find out what others think of it. Your co-worker, who goes to the movies at least twice a week, says it's one of the best films he's ever seen; he thinks you'll love it. Your sister, who knows you very well, says she thought it was OK, but she thinks you'll hate it. A review in the *Times* calls it "dull" and "uninspired," a "real disappointment." The full-page ad in the *Times*, however, calls it "dazzling," a "true cinematic triumph," and gives it "two thumbs up." What do you do?

In each of these instances, you're faced with opinions—what various people *think* about the movie. So whose opinion should you value most here? How do you make your decision?

DEFINITION: WHAT IS CREDIBILITY?

When you're faced with a batch of opinions to choose from, one of the most important things to consider is **credibility**. Credibility is the quality of being trustworthy and believable. The more credible (trustworthy, believable) your source, the more **valid** his or her opinion.

> **Credible:** able to be believed, trustworthy
> **Valid:** sound, well-founded, logical

A **valid** opinion is one that is sound, well-founded, and logical. To determine whether an opinion is valid—that is, to determine whether, and to what degree, a source is credible—there are three qualities to consider:

- Reliability
- Freedom from bias
- Expertise

These three factors are also very important when dealing with those tentative truths you encountered in the last lesson. Whenever you're offered opinions or facts that you aren't comfortable accepting but aren't able to verify, the credibility of your source is crucial in helping you decide whether or not to accept those opinions or tentative truths.

RELIABILITY

Reliability is a very desirable quality in a friend—and also in someone providing you with information. Just as you want your friends to be dependable, you want your sources of information to be dependable. That is, you want to know that they can be relied upon to give correct information.

> **Reliable:** dependable, truthful

When determining the reliability of your source, you're essentially measuring your degree of **confidence** in your source. The test for reliability is your past experience with the source and the source's reputation. Ask yourself the following questions:

1. Has this source been reliable in the past?
2. Does this source have a reputation for reliability?
3. Is there any reason to doubt the truthfulness or reliability of this source?

If you can answer "yes" to questions 1 and 2 and "no" to question 3, it is likely that you have a reliable source.

Though a source may have been reliable in the past, it's possible that you might have reason to doubt his or her reliability in the current situation. One of those reasons might be **bias**.

BIAS

Let's return to our movie-going scenario for a moment. In this situation, we have four different opinions to consider:

- What your co-worker thinks
- What your sister thinks
- What the *Times* review says
- What the *Times* ad says

Of the four, which is probably the *least* credible (least trustworthy) source, and why?

Common sense might tell you that the *Times* advertisement is the least credible source. Why? Precisely because it is an ad, and no advertisement is going to say anything bad about the product it's trying to sell, is it? Advertisements generally have a limited credibility because they're *biased*.

A **bias** is an opinion or feeling that strongly favors one side over others; a predisposition to support one side or a prejudice against other sides. The full-page ad in the *Times,* of course, has a vested interest in supporting the movie. No matter how good or how bad it really is, the ad is only going to print good comments so that you will go see the film.

Advertisers, of course, have a clear money-making agenda. But bias is often prevalent even in everyday situations. For example, you may be less likely to believe what your neighbor has to say about Candidate Warren simply because your neighbor keeps letting his dog go to the bathroom on your yard. In that case, you'd be influenced by your annoyance with your neighbor rather than the validity of his opinion. You need to remember to separate your feelings about your neighbor from what he actually has to say.

Similarly, another neighbor may have great things to say about Candidate Wilson, but if you know that this neighbor is Wilson's cousin, or that Wilson has promised your neighbor a seat on the local council, then you can see that your neighbor has something at stake in getting you to vote for Wilson. It's important, therefore, to know as much as possible about your sources when deciding how heavily to weigh their opinions.

PRACTICE

Consider the following scenario, and put a B next to anyone whom you think might be biased. If you think the person is likely to have an unbiased, reasonable opinion, put a U in the blank. The answers are given at the end of this lesson.

Situation: Congress is now debating a new tax reform proposal that makes filing taxes easier.

_____ **1.** The author of the proposal

_____ **2.** A professor of tax law

_____ **3.** A tax preparer

_____ **4.** The average taxpayer

EXPERTISE

Return again to the movie example. You've eliminated the *Times* ad because of bias, so you're now down to three possible choices: the opinions of your co-worker, your sister, and the *Times* review. How do you determine whose opinion is most credible? Once you establish reliability and identify any possible biases, you need to look for the next criterion: **expertise**.

Generally speaking, the greater a person's expertise—the more he or she knows about the subject—the more comfortable you should feel accepting his or her opinion. That is, in general, the greater the expertise, the greater the credibility.

In this situation, expertise falls into two areas: (1) knowledge of movies and (2) knowledge of you and your personal tastes. Thus, in order to determine credibility, you need to consider how much these three sources know both about what makes a good movie *and* how much these three sources know about what you enjoy in a film.

PRACTICE

Rank each of these three sources in each area of expertise on a scale of 1–3. Use 1 for the source with the most knowledge about the subject, and 3 for the source with the least. The answers are given at the end of the lesson.

5. Knowledge of movies:

_____ co-worker
_____ sister
_____ *Times* review

6. Knowledge of you and your taste in movies:

_____ co-worker
_____ sister
_____ *Times* review

DETERMINING LEVEL OF EXPERTISE

In many a courtroom, lawyers will call an "expert witness" to the stand to help their case. These expert witnesses are usually outside the case—that is, they are not involved in the alleged crime and do not have any relationship to or with the defendant; otherwise, they might be biased. For example, in a murder case where the defendant is pleading insanity, the lawyers might call upon psychologists who can provide expert opinions about the defendant's ability to distinguish between right and wrong.

For such testimony to be helpful to either side, however, the jury must be convinced that the expert witness is indeed an *expert*; they must be assured of his level of expertise, as well as his freedom from bias and his reliability. The lawyers will help establish the witness's level of expertise by providing information about the witness's:

- Education
- Experience
- Job or position
- Reputation
- Achievements

These five criteria are what you should look for when determining someone's level of expertise, and therefore credibility. One category is not necessarily more important than the other, though generally a person's education and experience carry the most weight.

An outstanding expert witness at this trial, therefore, might have the following profile:

Dr. John Francis
Education: Ph.D., Harvard University
Experience: 10 years at County Medical Hospital; 15 years at Harvard Psychiatric Center
Position: Currently Chief of Psychiatric Care at Harvard Psychiatric Center; teaches graduate courses at Harvard
Reputation: Ranked one of the 10 best on the east coast
Accomplishments: Has won several awards; was asked to serve on a federal judicial committee to establish guidelines for determining insanity; has written three textbooks and published 20 journal articles

Notice how strong Dr. Francis is in each of these five categories.

PRACTICE

Using the criteria for expertise, rank the choices below on a scale of 1–4 for credibility in the given situations. Use 1 for the person with most credibility, and 4 for the person with the least. The answers are given at the end of the lesson.

7. How to invest your inheritance from your great uncle
____ a. your great uncle's financial advisor
____ b. an investment banker
____ c. your favorite bank teller
____ d. *Investors Weekly* magazine

8. What kind of car you should buy

____ a.   your brother

____ b.   your mechanic

____ c.   *Consumer Reports*

____ d.   the car dealer nearest you

SPECIAL CASE: EYEWITNESS CREDIBILITY

One of the most difficult but important times to determine credibility is when there are eyewitnesses to a crime or other incident. Unfortunately, just because someone was at the scene doesn't mean his or her account is credible. One obvious factor that can interfere with witness credibility is, of course, bias. Let's say two co-workers, Andrea and Brady, get in a fight. There are three witnesses. Al is friends with Andrea; Bea is friends with Brady; and Cecil is friends with both Andrea and Brady. Chances are that what Al saw will favor Andrea and what Bea saw will favor Brady. What Cecil saw, however, will probably be closest to the unbiased truth.

Other factors besides bias can also interfere with witness credibility. If an incident occurs at a bar, for example, we have several possible interferences. It was probably dark, smoky, and noisy, and the witnesses may have been drinking, tired, or simply not paying very much attention to their surroundings.

Furthermore, the longer the time between the event and the time of questioning, the more unreliable the account of the witness will be. Think for a minute about your childhood. Did you ever tell a story about something that happened when you were little, only to be corrected by a parent or sibling who says, "That's not what happened"? Their version is different. Why?

Because our memory fades quickly and can be influenced by our own ideas about ourselves and others.

Thus, there are at least four factors that influence the credibility of eyewitnesses:

- Bias
- Environment
- Physical and emotional condition of the witness
- Time between event and recollection of event

PRACTICE

Pretend you are a police officer who has just arrived at the scene of a fight between two young men on a street corner. Three people witnessed the incident, which occurred at 9:00 P.M. You arrive and begin interviewing witnesses at 9:20 P.M. The street corner is well lit. (The answer is given at the end of the lesson.)

9. Who do you think is the most credible witness, and why?

Witness A is an elderly woman who was sitting on the stoop about ten feet from the corner. She was wearing her glasses, but she admits that she needs a stronger prescription. Her hearing, however, is fine. She doesn't know either boy involved in the incident, though she's seen them around the neighborhood before.

Witness B is a friend of one of the boys but does not know the other. He is an outstanding student at the local high school and a star basketball player. He was at the deli around the corner buying bread when he heard the boys shouting and came out to see what was going on. He had just had a fight with his girlfriend.

Witness C is a stranger to the neighborhood. He was crossing the street toward the corner when the boys started fighting. He has 20/20 vision. He is 45 and has two teenage children. He was only a few feet away from the boys when the fight occurred.

IN SHORT

When you're making decisions and solving problems, it's important to consider the credibility of your sources.

To determine whether a source is trustworthy, you must determine whether the source is reliable, consider the possibility that the source is biased, and evaluate the source's level of expertise. Expertise is determined by education, experience, job or position, reputation, and achievements. Eyewitness credibility, on the other hand, must take into consideration the witness's potential for bias, the environment, the condition of the witness, and the time lapse between the event and the witness's recollection of the event.

Skill Building Until Next Time

- As you talk to others today and hear their opinions and tentative truths, think about their credibility. What biases might they have, if any? What is their level of expertise? Remember, a source's credibility can change depending upon the subject matter of the claim.
- If you have access to cable TV, spend a few hours watching Court TV. As you watch, pay particular attention to how lawyers attempt to establish the credibility of their witnesses and undermine the credibility of their opponents' witnesses.

ANSWERS

1-B; 2-U; 3-B; 4-U. The author of the proposal (1), of course, has a vested interest in the proposal and in seeing that it is passed. A tax preparer (3), meanwhile, has a vested interest in the proposal being rejected, because if the reform makes filing taxes easier, he just might lose business. The professor (2) may have a definite opinion about the proposal, but chances are she's pretty objective—she doesn't win or lose by having the proposal passed or rejected (except, of course, as a taxpayer herself). And the average taxpayer (4) will probably like the proposal, and for good (valid) reasons, but not because of any bias.

5. **Knowledge of movies:** 1–*Times* review; 2–co-worker; and 3–sister. Even though your co-

worker may not be a professional movie critic like the writer of the *Times* review, he goes to enough movies to have some credibility as an expert. You may not agree with his criteria for what makes a good movie, but at least he should have some criteria.

6. **Knowledge of you and your taste in movies:** Probably 1–sister; 2–co-worker; and 3–*Times* review, though this can vary greatly. Where you rank the *Times* review depends entirely upon your past experience with the *Times*. If you've never read a *Times* review before, or you don't usually, then it should probably be ranked as the lowest in expertise here. However, if you regularly read the reviews, you may have found that

you generally agree with the opinions of the reviewer—that is, you usually like the movies that get good reviews and dislike the movies that get poor ones. In this case, you can rank the *Times* review first. On the other hand, you may have found that you generally disagree with the reviewers—that you usually like the movies that they don't. In that case, the *Times* review would be the lowest on your list.

7. **1–d; 2–a; 3–b; 4–c,** though it's a close call between 1 and 2. Here, *Investors Weekly* is ranked first because it is the least biased and probably most comprehensive source. Your great uncle's financial advisor, however, also has a very high level of expertise. Clearly he'd done a good job, since you received a substantial inheritance from your great uncle; he obviously believes in investing. The only hesitation in putting his advisor first is the potential for bias: He may want to have you as his client. That's also why the investment banker is ranked third. Though she may be quite knowledgeable, she, too, may have certain ideas and opinions specific to her business, and she probably wants you as a client. Also, because she's a banker, she may be more limited in her breadth of knowledge than a financial advisor. Finally, your favorite bank teller has several problems, the biggest being that her education and experience with investments are probably quite limited.

8. Your ranking here depends upon how much your brother knows about cars. If he has bought several cars in recent years, is the kind of guy who does his homework, and has a lifestyle and budget similar to yours, then his expertise will be pretty high. This is also true if he is a mechanic, runs a car dealership, or is otherwise in the car business (though we would hope that he would be honest with you and not try to convince you to buy the kind of car he sells—unless he truly believes it is the best for you). The other sources should be ranked in the following order: **1-c; 2-b; 3-d.** The car dealer, of course, is the most biased of the sources, and the salespeople may not know a great deal about makes and models of cars besides those on their lot.

9. Though **Witness C** may have been distracted by traffic, chances are he's the most credible eyewitness. He was heading toward the corner and was looking at the boys. He may not have been able to hear what happened in the beginning, but he should have been able to see exactly what occurred. His vision is perfect and there's no reason to suspect any bias.

   Witness A is probably next on the list. Though she may not have been able to see as clearly as **Witness C,** she was close enough to have heard what passed between the boys. Again, we have little reason to suspect bias.

   Witness B is probably the least credible witness. Though he has a good reputation, he has two strikes against him. The first is that he is friends with one of the boys, so he may be biased. The second is that he had just had a fight with his girlfriend, so he may have been distracted and not paying much attention.

L·E·S·S·O·N

WHAT'S IN A WORD?

LESSON SUMMARY

The words people use can have a powerful effect on their listeners. By choosing certain words instead of others or by phrasing questions in a way that directs your answers, people may try to influence you to think or react in a certain way. This lesson will show you how to recognize this kind of subtle persuasion.

ou have a cousin who likes to sky dive, mountain climb, and race cars. How would you describe him?

- Reckless
- Adventurous
- Free-spirited

As different as these words are, each one can be used to describe someone who does the above activities. The word you choose, of course, depends upon your opinion of these activities. Clearly, *free-spirited* is the most positive word; *adventurous* is more or less neutral; and *reckless* is downright negative. Your word choice will convey a certain image of your cousin—whether you intend it to or not.

Words are powerful, and they can influence us without us even realizing it. That's because they carry at least two layers of meaning: denotation and connotation. **Denotation** is a word's exact or dictionary meaning. **Connotation** is the implied or suggested meaning, the emotional impact that the word carries. For example, *thin, slender,* and *lean* all mean essentially the same thing—their denotation is the same—but they have different connotations. *Slender* suggests a gracefulness that *thin* and *lean* do not. *Lean,* on the other hand, suggests a hardness or scarcity that *thin* and *slender* do not.

Denotation: the dictionary meaning of a word
Connotation: the emotional impact or implied meaning of a word

---

Because words carry so much weight, advertisers, politicians, and anyone else who wants to convince you to believe one thing or another choose their words carefully. By using subtle persuasion techniques, they can often manipulate feelings and influence reactions so craftily that viewers and listeners don't realize it's happening. The best way to prevent this kind of influence is to be aware of these techniques. If you can recognize them, they lose their power. It's like watching a magician on stage once you already know the secret behind his tricks. You appreciate his art, but you're no longer under his spell.

There are three different subtle persuasion techniques we'll discuss in this lesson: *euphemisms, dysphemisms,* and *biased questions.*

EUPHEMISMS AND DYSPHEMISMS

Euphemisms are the most common of the subtle persuasion techniques. You've probably used them many times without even realizing it. A euphemism is when a word or phrase—usually one that's harsh, negative, or offensive—is replaced with a milder or more positive expression.

For example, imagine that you make a mistake in calculating the budget for a software development project. You could tell your boss that you made a mistake; however, if you want to downplay that mistake—that is, if you want to make it seem less of a problem—you'd be wise to choose a softer word, like *error* or, better yet, *miscalculation.* In each case, you're saying the same thing, but the word you choose conveys a different level of concern. Your boss will judge the severity of the error on its own merit, of course, but the word you use when you tell your boss about your mistake can help shape his or her attitude toward the whole situation.

It's often easy to spot euphemisms once you know what to look for, and the way politicians, advertisers, and others use euphemisms to avoid the truth can often be quite amusing. Not long ago, for example, Governor Christine Todd Whitman of New Jersey protested an automobile advertisement that pointed out, quite unapologetically, that on certain stretches of the New Jersey Turnpike, motorists must put up with a rather unpleasant odor. Attempting to downplay the existence of this odor, but unable to deny it, Whitman stretched her euphemistic wings and acknowledged that the air does indeed have an "olfactory impact."

Similarly, the automobile industry has used euphemisms to make us more inclined to consider buying a used car. Used cars, in fact, are no longer *used cars*—they're *previously owned vehicles,* a much more pleasant phrase but another obvious euphemism.

> **Euphemism:** a milder or more positive expression used to replace a negative or unpleasant one
>
> **Dysphemism:** replacing a neutral or positive expression with one that is negative or unpleasant

Other instances of euphemisms—and their opposites, **dysphemisms**—can be much more subtle. Take a look at the following sentences:

- They've decided to use the **standard** marketing approach.
- They've decided to use the **regulation** marketing approach.
- They've decided to use the **ordinary** marketing approach.
- They've decided to use the **usual** marketing approach.
- They've decided to use the **conventional** marketing approach.

Where euphemisms replace negative or neutral expressions with ones that are more positive, dysphemisms do the opposite: they replace positive or neutral expressions with ones that are negative or unpleasant. In the sentences above, it may not seem like one of the highlighted words is more negative or positive than the others; the sentences all seem to say almost exactly the same thing. However, each of the highlighted words has its own connotation, and the sentences could be ranked according to their positive and negative connotations. For example, *regulation* suggests a regimentation, a lack of freedom of choice. Similarly, *ordinary* suggests a lack of imagination or excitement. *Conventional* suggests an adherence to the status quo, while *standard* suggests a steadiness or reliability. Thus, we

might rank the sentences, from most positive to most negative, as follows:

1. They've decided to use the **usual** marketing approach.
2. They've decided to use the **standard** marketing approach.
3. They've decided to use the **conventional** marketing approach.
4. They've decided to use the **ordinary** marketing approach.
5. They've decided to use the **regulation** marketing approach.

> **Euphemisms** and **dysphemisms**—subtle and otherwise—are used a great deal in political and social issues. If you oppose abortion, for example, then you are *pro-life* rather than *anti-choice* or *anti-abortion*. If you support the right to abort, on the other hand, you're *pro-choice* rather than *anti-life* or *pro-abortion*. See how important these euphemisms are? How could someone be *against* life? *Against* choice?

PRACTICE

Take each of the neutral words or phrases below and try to come up with a euphemism and dysphemism for each. The answers are given at the end of this lesson.

1. Assassination

2. Stalemate

3. Problem

Read the following sentences carefully. Then rewrite the sentence, replacing the italicized word or phrase with a euphemism or dysphemism. Example: Charles was *let*

EXAMPLES OF EUPHEMISMS AND DYSPHEMISMS

Neutral Word or Phrase	Euphemism	Dysphemism
death penalty	capital punishment	government subsidized murder
inexpensive	economical	cheap
affair	romance	cuckoldry
rebel	freedom fighter	insurgent

go. A: Charles was canned. B: Charles was offered an opportunity for a career transition.

_____ **4.** Please don't *worry* about something so *minor.*

_____ **5.** He's a *clever* fellow.

_____ **6.** As part of the redevelopment of Spring Lakes, current residents will be *relocated* so that a shopping mall can be built.

BIASED QUESTIONS

Imagine someone stops you on the street and asks you to participate in a survey about euthanasia. You agree, and she asks you the following questions:

- Do you support the murder of the terminally ill?
- Do you believe doctors should have the right to kill elderly people in pain?

No matter how you really feel about euthanasia, chances are you can't answer anything but *no* to these questions. Why? Because if you say *yes*, it sounds like you support the murder of the elderly. The way these questions are phrased—and the words that are used—make it difficult for you to give a fair answer. That is,

the questions themselves express a certain attitude toward euthanasia, and that *prejudices* the questions. In short, the questions aren't fair. They're biased.

Notice how these particular questions use dysphemisms to bias the questions and push you to answer a certain way. Here, *euthanasia* becomes *murder of the terminally ill* and *perform assisted suicide* becomes *kill.*

Here is how the questions might be revised to express the opposing point of view:

- Do you support efforts to ease the pain and suffering of the terminally ill?
- Do you believe doctors have the right to end the pain of the elderly at their request?

Notice how answering *yes* to these questions is much easier than answering *no.* If you say *no,* especially to the first, you may seem less than compassionate, indifferent to the pain and suffering of the terminally ill. In the example above, euphemisms are used to bias the questions in the opposite direction.

Here are the questions revised once again so that you can answer *yes* or *no* fairly:

- Do you support euthanasia?
- Do you believe doctors should have the right to administer euthanasia?

Professional surveys will be careful to ask fair questions, but when political organizations, advertisers, and other groups or individuals have a certain agenda, they may use biased questions to get certain results. Similarly, anyone who wants to influence you may use biased questions to get you to respond in a certain way. That's why it's important for you to recognize when a question is fair and when it's biased.

PRACTICE

Read the following questions carefully. If you think the question is biased, write a B in the blank. If you think it's unbiased, write a U. Answers are given at the end of this lesson.

_____ **7.** What did you think of that lousy movie?

_____ **8.** How do you feel about capital punishment?

_____ **9.** Are you going to vote to re-elect that crooked politician for governor?

_____ **10.** Do you support the gun control laws that limit our freedom and our Constitutional right to bear arms?

_____ **11.** Should medical marijuana be legalized?

PRACTICE

To further improve your critical thinking and reasoning skills, take each of the unbiased questions from the previous exercise and turn them into biased questions. Then do the opposite: take the biased questions and turn them into fair questions. Write your answers on a separate piece of paper. Sample answers are given at the end of this lesson.

IN SHORT

Euphemisms, dysphemisms, and _biased questions_ can have a powerful influence on readers and listeners. Euphemisms replace negative expressions with ones that are neutral or positive. Dysphemisms do the opposite: they replace neutral or positive expressions with ones that are harsh or negative. Biased questions make it difficult for us to answer questions fairly. Learning to recognize these subtle persuasion techniques promotes independent thinking and lets people come to their own conclusions, rather than the conclusions others want them to reach.

Skill Building Until Next Time

- Listen carefully to conversations, to the news, to what people say to you and ask of you. Do you notice any euphemisms, dysphemisms, or biased questions? Did you catch yourself using any of these techniques yourself?
- You can improve your ability to recognize subtle persuasion techniques by practicing them yourself. Come up with euphemisms, dysphemisms, and biased questions throughout the day.

ANSWERS

There are many possible answers. Here are a few:

Euphemism	Dysphemism
1. neutralization, termination	murder
2. impasse, draw	dead end
3. challenge	mess

4. Please don't *fuss* over a *trifle*. (dysphemism)

5. He's a *crafty* fellow. (dysphemism) **or** He's a *shrewd* fellow. (euphemism)

6. As part of the redevelopment of Spring Lakes, current residents will be *uprooted* so that a shopping mall can be built. (dysphemism)

7. B. The word *lousy* makes it hard to say you liked it; you'd be admitting to liking lousy films. *What did you think of that movie?*

8. U. Unless you think *capital punishment* is a euphemism for *death penalty*, in which case this is slightly biased. *Don't you think that the death penalty is the only fair punishment for murderers?*

9. B. Who in their right mind would vote for a crooked politician? *Are you going to vote to re-elect the governor?*

10. B. Again, clearly biased. A *yes* answer means you want to restrict freedom and contradict the Constitution. *Do you support gun control?*

11. U. *Do you think that medical marijuana, which dramatically relieves the pain and suffering of cancer and glaucoma patients, should be legalized?*

L·E·S·S·O·N
WORKING WITH ARGUMENTS
6

LESSON SUMMARY

You hear arguments of all kinds throughout the day. In this lesson, you'll learn how to recognize the components of a deductive argument and how it differs from an inductive argument.

C onsider the following conversation:
"Junior, time to go to bed."
"But why?"
"Because I said so!"

Parents often get away with giving the answer "because I said so." But even young children sense the unfairness of the argument. Critical thinkers know that it's important to provide good reasons when asking someone to accept a claim or take a certain action. Providing good reasons means *supporting* your argument.

In the next three lessons, you're going to learn about **deductive arguments**: what they are, how they work, how to recognize misleading arguments, and how to recognize (and make) a good deductive argument—one that supports its assertions.

First, you need to know what *deductive reasoning* is. To help define it, the counterpart of deductive reasoning, which is *inductive reasoning*, will be introduced first.

Knowing the difference between these two types of reasoning and knowing what makes a good inductive and deductive argument are very important tools for the critical thinker. Whether you're negotiating a pay raise, trying to convince others to support your cause or buy your product, or demonstrating that your experiment's results are valid, you're making an argument—and you need to know how to make a good one. Similarly, knowing the structure of inductive and deductive arguments (and what makes them valid) will enable you to assess other people's arguments and make more effective and logical decisions.

INDUCTIVE REASONING

When detectives arrive at the scene of a crime, the first thing they do is look for clues that can help them piece together what happened. A broken window, for example, might suggest how a burglar entered—or exited. Likewise, the fact that the intruder didn't disturb anything but the picture that hid the safe might suggest that the burglar knew exactly where the safe was hidden. And this, in turn, suggests that the burglar knew the victim.

The process described above is called **inductive reasoning.** It consists of:

1. Making observations, and then
2. Drawing conclusions from those observations

Like a detective, you use inductive reasoning all the time in your daily life. You might notice, for example, that every time you eat a hot dog with chili and onions, you get a stomach ache. Using inductive reasoning, you could logically conclude that the chili dogs cause indigestion—and that you should probably stop eating them. Similarly, you might notice that your lab partner scowls at you every time you call him "Tony." You could logically conclude that he doesn't like that nickname and

that you should address him as "Anthony." In both examples, what you're doing is moving from the *specific*—a particular observation—to the *general*—a larger conclusion. Inductive reasoning starts from observation and evidence and leads to a conclusion.

Using inductive reasoning generally involves the following questions:

1. What have you observed? What evidence is available?
2. What can you conclude from that evidence?
3. Is that *conclusion* logical?

These questions will be addressed in a later lesson. For now, you know enough about inductive reasoning to see how deductive reasoning is different.

DEDUCTIVE REASONING

Unlike inductive reasoning, which moves from *specific evidence* to a *general conclusion*, **deductive reasoning** does the opposite; it generally works from a *conclusion* to the *evidence* for that conclusion. In inductive reasoning, the conclusion has to be "figured out" and we must determine whether or not the conclusion is valid. In deductive reasoning, on the other hand, we start with the conclusion and then see if the *evidence* for that conclusion is valid. Generally, if the evidence is valid, the conclusion it supports is valid as well. In other words, deductive reasoning involves asking:

1. What is the conclusion?
2. What evidence supports it?
3. Is that *evidence* logical?

If you can answer *yes* to question 3, then the conclusion should be logical and the argument is sound.

It's easy to confuse inductive and deductive reasoning, so here's a little mneumonic device to help you remember which is which:

Deductive: Conclusion ➔ Evidence (DCE)
Inductive: Evidence ➔ Conclusion (IEC)

You can remember that the word *Deductive* begins with a consonant, and so does *Conclusion*, which is where you begin in deductive reasoning. Similarly, *Inductive* begins with a vowel, as does *Evidence*, so in inductive reasoning, you start with the evidence.

In the field of logic, deductive reasoning includes *formal* (mathematical or symbolic) logic such as syllogisms and truth tables. Some practice with formal logic will certainly sharpen your critical thinking and reasoning skills, but this book won't cover that kind of logic. Instead, we will continue to focus on *informal* logic— that is, the kind of critical thinking and reasoning skills that help you solve problems, assess and defend arguments, and make effective decisions in your daily life.

THE PARTS OF A DEDUCTIVE ARGUMENT

Lesson 2, "Problem Solving Strategies," talked about the importance of identifying the main issue in order to solve a problem. You learned to ask yourself, "What is the real problem to be solved here?" Then you took that problem and broke it down into its parts.

In looking at deductive arguments, you should follow a similar process. First, you should identify the conclusion. The **conclusion** is the main claim or point the argument is trying to make. The various pieces of evidence that support that conclusion are called **premises**. Keep in mind that an argument is not necessarily a fight. In terms of inductive and deductive reasoning, an **argument** is any claim that is supported by evidence. Whether or not that evidence is good is another matter.

Identifying the conclusion is often more difficult than you might expect, because conclusions can sometimes seem like premises, and vice versa. Another difficulty is that you're used to thinking of conclusions as coming at the end of something. But in deductive arguments, the conclusion can pop up anywhere. Thus, when someone presents you with a deductive argument, the first thing you should do is ask: "What is the main claim, or overall idea, that the argument is trying to prove?"

In other words, just as a problem is often composed of many smaller problems, the conclusion in a deductive argument is often composed of many premises. So it's important to keep in mind the "big picture."

Claim:	assertion about the truth, existence, or value of something
Argument:	any claim that is supported by evidence
Conclusion:	the main or overall claim in an argument
Premises:	the claims that support the conclusion

THE STRUCTURE OF DEDUCTIVE ARGUMENTS

The premises that support the conclusion in a deductive argument can have two different structures. In one type of deductive argument, **separate support,** each premise provides its own *individual support* of the conclusion. That is, each premise alone is evidence for that main claim. In the other type of argument, **chain of support,** the premises work together to support the conclusion. That is, they work like a chain of ideas to support the argument. These two types of arguments are represented as diagrams on the next page:

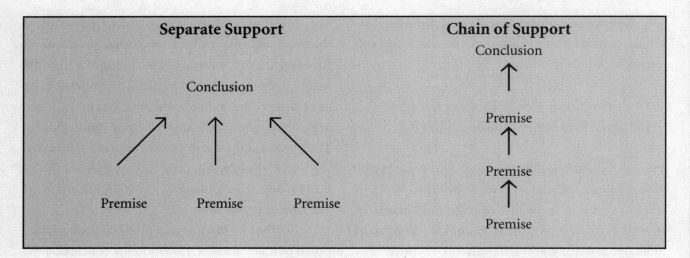

Here's how these two structures might look in a real argument:

Separate support: You shouldn't take that job. The pay is lousy, the hours are terrible, and there are no benefits.

You shouldn't take that job.

↑   ↑   ↑

The pay   The hours   There are
is lousy.   are terrible.   no benefits.

Chain support: You shouldn't take that job. The pay is lousy, which will make it hard for you to pay your bills, and that will make you unhappy.

You shouldn't take that job.

↑

and that will make you unhappy

↑

which will make it hard for you to pay your bills

↑

the pay is lousy

Notice how in the second version, the entire argument builds upon one idea, the lousy pay, whereas in the first, the argument is built upon three ideas. Both arguments, however, are equally logical.

Of course, an argument can have both separate and chain support. We'll see an example of that shortly. What's important now is to understand that when premises depend upon each other, as they do in the chain support structure, what we really have is a chain of premises and conclusions. Look how the layers of a chain support argument work:

Overall conclusion:	You shouldn't take that job.
Premise:	That will make you unhappy.
Conclusion:	That will make you unhappy.
Premise:	It will be hard to pay your bills.
Conclusion:	It will be hard to pay your bills.
Premise:	The pay is lousy.

Because deductive arguments often work this way, it's extra important to be able to distinguish the *overall* conclusion from the conclusions that may be used in the chain of support.

IDENTIFYING THE OVERALL CONCLUSION

Take a good look at the following sentences:

He's rich, so he must be happy. All rich people are happy.

These two sentences represent a small deductive argument. It's not a particularly *good* argument, but it is a good example of deductive structure. If these two sentences are broken down into their parts, three different claims arise:

1. He's rich.
2. He must be happy.
3. All rich people are happy.

Now ask the key question: "What is this argument trying to prove?" In other words, what is the conclusion here?

Two clues should help you come up with the right answer. First look at which claims have support (evidence) in this example. Is there anything here to support the claim that "He is rich"? No. Is there anything to support the claim that "All rich people are happy"? No again. But there *are* premises to support the claim that "He must be happy." Why must he be happy? Because:

1. He is rich.
2. All rich people are happy.

Therefore, the conclusion of this argument is "He must be happy." That is what the writer is trying to prove. The premises that support this conclusion are "He is rich" and "All rich people are happy."

A second clue that "He must be happy" is the conclusion is the word *so*. In deductive arguments, several key words and phrases indicate that a conclusion will follow. Similarly, certain words and phrases indicate that a premise will follow:

Indicate a Conclusion:
- Accordingly
- As a result
- Consequently
- Hence
- It follows that
- So
- That's why
- Therefore
- This shows/means/suggests that
- Thus

Indicate a Premise:
- As indicated by
- As shown by
- Because
- For
- Given that
- Inasmuch as
- Since
- The reason is that

Now that you've identified the conclusion, are the premises that support that conclusion separate support or chain support?

You should be able to see that these premises *work together* to support the conclusion. "He is rich" alone doesn't support the conclusion, and neither does "All rich people are happy." But the two premises together provide support for the conclusion. Thus, the example is considered a *chain of support* argument.

THE POSITION OF THE CONCLUSION

While you might be used to thinking of the conclusion as something that comes at the end, in a deductive argument, the conclusion can move around. Here is the same argument rearranged in several different ways:

- He must be happy. After all, he's rich, and all rich people are happy.

- All rich people are happy. Since he's rich, he must be happy.
- He's rich, and all rich people are happy. He must be happy.
- He must be happy. After all, all rich people are happy, and he's rich.
- All rich people are happy. He must be happy because he's rich.

In larger deductive arguments, especially the kind found in articles and essays, the conclusion will often be stated before any premises. In fact, you'll often be expected to use this structure when writing essays: your introduction should express your thesis (conclusion) and the body of the essay should support that thesis (premises). But it's important to remember that the conclusion can appear anywhere in an argument. The key is to keep in mind what the argument *as a whole* is trying to prove.

One way to test that you've found the right conclusion is to use the "because" test. If you've chosen the right claim, you should be able to put *because* between it and all of the other premises. Thus:

He must be happy **because** he's rich and **because** all rich people are happy.

PRACTICE

Read the following short arguments carefully. First, separate the arguments into claims by putting a slash mark (/) between each claim. Then, identify the claim that represents the *conclusion* in each deductive argument by underlining that claim. Finally, for each argument, identify whether the premises work as separate support or chain support. Answers are given at the end of this lesson.

Example: Facial expressions are a universal language. Cultures all around the world recognize the smile of happiness and the scowl of anger. The faces we make to express joy, fear, anger, sadness, surprise, and disgust are all the same in all parts of the globe.

<u>Facial expressions are a universal language.</u> / Cultures all around the world recognize the smile of happiness and the scowl of anger. / The faces we make to express joy, fear, anger, sadness, surprise, and disgust are all the same in all parts of the globe.

1. Our competitors have lowered their prices. We'd better lower ours, too. Our sales are down and our inventory is high.

2. She's smart and she has integrity. She'd make a great councilwoman. You should vote for her.

3. I don't think you should drive. You'd better give me the keys. You had a lot to drink tonight.

4. You really should stop smoking. Smoking causes lung cancer and emphysema. It makes your clothes and breath smell like smoke. Besides, it's a waste of money.

IN SHORT

Unlike inductive arguments, which move from evidence to conclusion, deductive arguments move from the conclusion to evidence for that conclusion. The **conclusion** is the overall claim or main point of the argument, and the claims that support the conclusion are called **premises.** Deductive arguments can be supported by premises that work alone (separate support) or together (chain of support).

Skill Building Until Next Time

- When you hear an argument, ask yourself whether it is an inductive or deductive argument. Did the person move from evidence to conclusion, or conclusion to evidence? If the argument is too complex to analyze this way, try choosing just one part of the argument and see whether it's inductive or deductive.
- When you come across deductive arguments today, try to separate the conclusion from the premises. Then consider whether the premises are separate or chain support.

ANSWERS

Before you check your answers below, use the "because" test to see if you've correctly identified the conclusion.

1. Our competitors have lowered their prices./ <u>We'd better lower ours, too.</u> Our sales are down/ and our inventory is high.
   Separate. Three separate premises support the conclusion.

2. She's smart / and she has integrity. / She'd make a great councilwoman. / <u>You should vote for her.</u>
   Separate and chain. "She's smart" and "she has integrity" are two separate claims that support the premise "She'd make a great councilwoman." That premise, in turn, supports the conclusion.

3. I don't think you should drive. / <u>You'd better give me the keys.</u> / You had a lot to drink tonight.
   Chain. The last premise, "You had a lot to drink tonight," supports the first, which in turn supports the conclusion.

4. <u>You really should stop smoking</u>. / Smoking causes lung cancer and emphysema. / It makes your clothes and breath smell like smoke. / Besides, it's a waste of money.
   Separate. Three separate premises support the conclusion.

7

PARTIAL CLAIMS AND HALF-TRUTHS

LESSON SUMMARY

Every day we're bombarded with arguments aimed at getting us to buy a product or support a cause. This lesson will show you how to recognize incomplete claims and hidden agendas in those arguments.

You're relaxing on your sofa watching your favorite television show when it's time for a commercial break. Suddenly a handsome announcer comes on the screen and tells you that new Stain-Ex laundry detergent out-performs the leading brand, *and* it costs less! Sounds like a great product. But should you run out and buy it?

Well, besides the fact that you're probably quite comfortable on your couch, the answer is no—at least not yet. Not until you investigate further.

THE TROUBLE WITH INCOMPLETE CLAIMS

Why shouldn't you go out and buy Stain-Ex? After all, it "out-performs the leading brand" *and* "it costs less!" So what's the problem?

The problem is that while the announcer's claims *sound* like facts, they're really quite misleading—and meant to be. Maybe Stain-Ex did "out-perform" the leading brand (which brand is that?)—but in what category?

Stain removing? Whitening? Brightening? Sudsing? Rinsing? Smell? The ad doesn't say. The claim *sounds* good, but because it is incomplete, you don't know *what* it's claiming. And until you determine exactly what it's claiming, it's difficult to accept it even as a tentative truth.

Furthermore, the commercial claims that Stain-Ex "costs less." Because the first claim compares Stain-Ex to the leading brand, it's easy to assume that Stain-Ex costs less than the *leading brand*. But is that what the ad really says? If you aren't listening carefully, it's easy to hear what you want to hear, or rather, what the makers of Stain-Ex want you to hear. The commercial simply says that Stain-Ex "costs less." It never specifies less than *what*. To assume it costs less than the leading brand is to fall right into the ad's trap. This type of argument—where the premises are misleading or incomplete claims—may be good for Stain-Ex, but not so good for you or the leading brand.

Flip through just about any popular magazine and you'll find page after page of advertisements that make this kind of incomplete claim to make you think their product, service, or idea is something that it's not. These ads may use unclear words or phrases, leave out essential information, or compare incomparable items. For example, you might see an ad claiming that new Crispy Potato Chips have one-third the fat per serving of Munch Chips. Sounds good, right? But what important information has been left out? What do you need to know to determine whether or not this is a fair comparison?

What the ad leaves out, of course, is the serving size. Without that information, how do you know it's a fair comparison? Maybe a serving of Crispy Chips is two ounces, whereas a serving of Munch Chips is six ounces. In that case, Crispy Chips is just as fattening as Munch Chips.

Similarly, A-Plus Test Prep Service may argue that it's the best test-prep company in town. After all, its clients "perform 50% better on MCATs and LSATs." But this premise is flawed. Fifty percent better than what? A-Plus hopes we'll fill in the blank for them—50% better than people who haven't used A-Plus—but that premise is merely *implied*, not stated. It could be 50% better than seventh graders. Truth is, we don't know.

To ensure that the decisions you make are really your own, you need to be particularly aware of the argument structure in advertisements and other persuasive sources. These arguments typically have one or more of the following weak points.

Their premises:

1. Use unclear words or phrases
2. Leave out important information
3. Compare incomparable items

In other words, their premises are only partial claims or half-truths. As a critical thinker, you need to look carefully at these arguments, identify the conclusion, and then determine whether any of the premises (or even the conclusion itself) suffer from one or more of these weaknesses. If so, you should think twice about accepting the conclusion until you can get more information.

PRACTICE

Below are several incomplete claims and comparisons. Rewrite them so that they're complete. Possible answers are given at the end of this lesson.

Example:
Incomplete claim: Now with 20% more flavor!
Revised claim: Now with 20% more onion flavor than our old recipe!

1. Incomplete claim: Energy Batteries last longer!

Revised claim:

2. Incomplete claim: New and improved Mildew-Gone is tougher.

Revised claim:

3. Incomplete claim: Smooth-Touch toilet tissue—twice the paper at half the price!

Revised claim:

TESTS AND STUDIES

The makers of the Stain-Ex commercial know you're onto them, so they've remade their commercial. Now the announcer tells you:

Studies show that new Stain-Ex out-performs the leading brand in laboratory tests. And it costs less per fluid ounce than Tidy!

Well, they've certainly fixed their "costs less" claim. But what about their tests? Can you now safely believe that Stain-Ex is a better detergent than the leading brand? Have they now presented a good argument?

Not necessarily. Again, what the ad says *sounds* great, but you have to remember that this *is* an ad, which means you have to question its credibility. Your questions should be all the more insistent because the ad doesn't tell you anything *about* the tests. You don't know, for example:

- Who conducted the studies?
- How were the studies conducted?
- What exactly was tested?
- What exactly were the results?

We'll spend a whole lesson talking about tests and studies later in the book. For now, however, it's important to remember that tests and studies can be manipulated to get certain results. In other words, it's important to have a healthy skepticism about tests, surveys, and studies. They should only be accepted as very tentative truths until you can find out the answers to the kind of questions we ask above.

For example, advertiser Bob can say that "4 out of 5 dentists surveyed recommend CleanRight toothpaste to their patients." In order for this claim to be true, all he has to do is survey 5 dentists—4 of whom are his friends and who he knows *do* recommend that toothpaste. Is Bob's survey fair? Certainly not. But he can now make this claim, and it sounds awfully good to the consumer.

Probably the most important consideration is *who* conducted the study. Why? Because knowing who conducts it can determine whether or not it's legitimate. Do the conductors have anything at stake in the results? For example, if an independent consumer group conducted the Stain-Ex lab tests, would you feel better about accepting their claims as tentative truths? Absolutely; they're more credible because they're not very likely to be biased. But if Stain-Ex itself conducted the tests, the likelihood of bias is extremely high—it's better to be highly skeptical about that claim.

In the real world, of course, it's a little more complicated than this, but you get the idea; studies and surveys are not always to be trusted.

PRACTICE

Read the following claims carefully. Which are complete and credible (C)? Which are incomplete or incredible (I)? Answers are given at the end of this lesson.

_____**4.** Recent taste tests prove Rich Chocolate Frosting tastes best.

_____**5.** According to a Temple University study, 3 out of 5 Philadelphia shoppers surveyed have used their debit cards instead of cash to pay for groceries at their local supermarkets.

_____**6.** A recent survey shows Americans prefer Choco-Bites to regular chocolate chip cookies.

AVERAGES

Imagine you recently heard someone on a talk show claim that "the average American teenager spends 29 hours per week watching television." This claim should trouble you for two reasons: first, because 29 hours a week is _far_ too much television, and second, because of the way the claim uses the word _average. Average_ is a word that is often misused, and often used to mislead.

DEFINING "AVERAGE"

In the claim above, the problem with the word _average_ is its definition.

What _is_ the "average" or typical American teenager like? What age? What habits? What likes or dislikes? How we define "the average American teenager" can make a big difference in what this claim actually means.

Sometimes using the word _average_ to describe something is good enough—like the _average banana_ for example. But often an average something is in the eye of the beholder. My definition of an average teenager, for example, is probably quite different from my parents' definition, and both of our definitions are probably quite different from my 15-year-old cousin's idea of the average teen.

As a critical thinker, you should be on the lookout for vague uses of the word _average._ Unless it is followed by a definition of what that average population is like, you should be hesitant to accept the claim.

NUMERICAL AVERAGES

The word _average_ can also be troublesome when we're talking about numbers. Take, for example, the following advertisement:

Looking for a safe, secure place to start a family? Then come to Serenity, Virginia. With an average of ten acres per lot, our properties provide your children with plenty of space to grow and play. Our spacious lawns, tree-lined streets, and friendly neighbors make Serenity a great place to grow up!

Sounds like a terrific place, doesn't it? Unfortunately, this ad is very misleading if you think you're going to move onto a big property.

In most cases, **average** means _mean_, the number reached by dividing the total number by the number of participants. Let's take a look at how Serenity came up with this number. Here are the facts:

In Serenity, there are 100 properties. Ten of those properties have 91 acres each. Ninety of those properties have only 1 acre each.

$$10 \times 91 = 910$$
$$90 \times 1 = \underline{90}$$

1000	(total acres)
÷ 100	(number of properties)
10	(average acres per property)

Ten acres is the average, all right. But does that represent the majority? Does the average accurately suggest what most properties in Serenity are like? Obviously not. In Serenity, the typical house sits on just one acre, not ten.

It's important to keep in mind that *average* does not necessarily mean *typical* or *usual*. Unfortunately, that's generally what people think of when they hear the word *average*. And that's why an ad like this can be so misleading.

The fact is, when it comes to numerical averages, there are actually *three* different possible averages to calculate. There's the **mean**, which is what the folks in Serenity used to come up with their figure, but there's also the **median** and the **mode**. Here are definitions of the three types of averages.

> **Mean:** the value reached by adding the numbers and dividing that total by the number of participants or quantities
>
> **Median:** the value that is in the middle: half of the quantities are above and half are below
>
> **Mode:** the value that is the most common or that appears the most often

Thus, if you compare the mean and mode for property size in Serenity, you can see just how different "average" can be:

Property size in Serenity, VA:

Mean:	10 acres
Mode:	1 acre

In other words, Serenity's ad would be much closer to the truth if it had used the mode instead of the mean.

Similarly, you could compare the averages for age of the head of household in a particular town and see a vast difference:

Average age of head of household, Cedar Oaks, WI:

Mean:	35
Median:	54
Mode:	42

These numbers suggest several things. Because the mean is much lower than the median, we can conclude that there are probably a lot of heads of household in their early twenties in Cedar Oaks. The median tells us, however, that there are also a good number of older folks in Cedar Oaks, since half of the heads of household are older than 54. And the mode tells us that if you were to go door to door asking the heads of household how old they were, you'd hear "42" more than any other number. But be careful: that does *not* mean that most Cedar Oaks heads of household are 42 years old. It simply means that of all the ages, that age appears most often.

PRACTICE

Read the following claims carefully to determine whether the use of the word *average* is acceptable or problematic. If the word is problematic, explain why. Answers are given at the end of this lesson.

7. The average woman lives a happier life than the average man.

8. The average life span of American women is two years longer than that of Canadian women.

9. The average salary at Wyntex Corporation is $75,000.

IN SHORT

Incomplete claims and half-truths can *look* and *sound* very convincing. But as a critical thinker, you have to be wary of such claims. When someone is trying to convince you to do something—as advertisers do hundreds of time each day, for instance—watch out for misleading claims that make their case sound stronger than it really is.

Skill Building Until Next Time

- Pick up a popular magazine and look for ads that make incomplete claims. Compare them to ads that show more respect for your judgment and give you more information.
- Listen carefully to others today at work, on the radio, on TV. Do you hear any incomplete claims? Do you notice any suspicious "averages"?

ANSWERS

Answers will vary. Below are some possible revisions:

1. Energy Batteries last two hours longer than For-ever Last!

2. New and improved Mildew-Gone is tougher on mildew stains than our old formula.

3. Smooth-Touch toilet tissue—twice as much paper as Thompson tissue at half the price per roll!

4. I. First of all, the validity of the taste tests should be questioned. Who conducted them? How? What exactly were the results? Second, "tastes best" is a vague phrase.

5. C. This claim is OK. More information about the study could be given, but because it's a university study of supermarkets, there's little chance for bias. Furthermore, the claim acknowledges that it's only

3 out of 5 shoppers *surveyed*. That is, they're not trying to suggest that they surveyed everyone.

6. I. This claim has several problems. First is the vagueness of the statement "a recent survey." Second, what are "regular" chocolate chip cookies?

7. Very problematic. What is the "average" woman? The "average" man? Furthermore, how do you define "happier"? Happier in what way?

8. Acceptable.

9. Problematic. The salary range at a company like Wyntex can be so large that $75,000 may not represent the typical salary. If the president and CEO make $2 billion a year, for example, that clearly inflates the average. Meanwhile, most employees at the company may be making less than $40,000.

L·E·S·S·O·N 8

EVALUATING EVIDENCE

LESSON SUMMARY

Since it's the *evidence* in a deductive argument that makes the conclusion valid, it's important to evaluate that evidence. This lesson will show you how to check premises for two key factors: credibility and reasonableness.

N ow that you're able to separate the conclusion from the premises that support it, it's time to *evaluate* those premises. This is a vital step; the conclusion, after all, is trying to convince you of something—that you should accept a certain opinion, change your beliefs, act in a certain way, or do a certain thing. Before you accept that conclusion, therefore, you need to examine the *validity* of the evidence for that conclusion.

Specifically, there are three questions to ask yourself when evaluating evidence:

1. What type of evidence is offered?
2. Is that evidence *credible?*
3. Is that evidence *reasonable?*

TYPES OF EVIDENCE

There are many different types of evidence that can be offered in support of a conclusion. One of the most basic distinctions to make is between premises that are fact, premises that are opinion, and premises that can only be accepted as tentative truths.

Before going any further, here's a review of the difference between fact and opinion:

- A **fact** is something known for certain to have happened, to be true, or to exist.
- An **opinion** is something believed to have happened, to be true, or to exist.
- A **tentative truth** is a claim that may be a fact but that you are not able to verify.

Whether they're facts, opinions, or tentative truths, premises can come in the following forms:

- Statistics or figures
- Physical evidence (artifacts)
- Things seen, felt, or heard (observations)
- Statements from experts and expert witnesses
- Reports of experiences
- Ideas, feelings, or beliefs

Of course, some types of evidence seem more convincing than others. That is, people are often more likely to believe or be convinced by statistics than by someone's opinion. But that doesn't mean that all statistics should automatically be accepted and that all opinions should be rejected. Because statistics can be manipulated and because opinions can be quite reasonable, *all* forms of evidence need to be carefully examined for both credibility and reasonableness.

The questions of credibility and reasonableness apply to different types of evidence to different degrees.

For example, the *reasonableness* of statistics can't really be questioned, but their *credibility* must be questioned. Similarly, any feeling or belief should be examined for both credibility *and* reasonableness.

IS THE EVIDENCE CREDIBLE?

Before you consider the credibility of the evidence the arguer offers, it's important to consider the credibility of the *arguer*. Is the person making the argument credible? Then, if the arguer offers evidence from other sources, the credibility of those sources needs to be questioned. If both the arguer and his or her sources seem credible, then the argument can tentatively be accepted. If not, the argument shouldn't be accepted until it is examined further.

First, here's a review of the criteria that determine credibility. To be credible, a source must:

- Be reliable
- Be free of bias
- Be an expert

Expertise is determined by:

- Education
- Experience
- Job or position
- Reputation
- Achievements

In the case of an eyewitness, the following must also be considered:

- The witness's potential for bias
- The environment
- The physical and mental condition of the witness

- The time between the event and recollection of the event

Below is a short deductive argument. Read the following passage from a student essay carefully:

Some people argue that "guns don't kill people—people kill people." But if we didn't have so many guns on the street, people wouldn't be able to kill other people so easily. That's why we must support gun control. Last year alone, over 10,000* children were killed by guns. My own brother was one of those victims. He was just walking down the street when he was killed by a stray bullet. Please, don't let this happen to your family.

*This and other statistics and in the rest of the text are fictitious and meant to serve purely as examples.

First, identify the conclusion in this passage. What is the overall claim or point that the passage is trying to prove? Once you identify the conclusion, underline it.

You should have underlined the claim "we must support gun control." The phrase "That's why" may have helped you identify this idea as the main claim. (If you had trouble, take a moment to review Lesson 6, "Working with Arguments.") Below is a table with a list of the premises that support this conclusion. Note that not every sentence in this argument is a premise.

The arguer's experience offers an important clue here about *her* credibility. Because of what happened to her brother, is she likely to be biased on the issue of gun control? Absolutely. However, does this rule her out as a credible arguer? Not necessarily. Chances are that if she lost her brother to gun violence, she knows more about the issue than the average person. In other words, her experience indicates that she has some level of expertise in the area. Thus, though there's evidence of some bias, there's also evidence of some expertise. Because there is both bias and expertise, the argument needs to be examined further before you can determine whether or not to accept it.

The next step is to consider the credibility of premises provided by the outside source; that is, the statistic offered about how many children have been killed by guns. Notice that here the arguer doesn't give a source for the figure that she provides. This should automatically ring an alarm. Because numbers can so easily be manipulated and misleading, it's crucial to know the source of any figures offered in support of an argument and assess the credibility of that source.

PREMISES THAT SUPPORT THE CONCLUSION

Type of Premise	Premise
Opinion	If we didn't have so many guns on the street, people wouldn't be able to kill other people so easily.
Statistic	Last year alone, over 10,000 children were killed by guns.
Experience	My own brother was one of those victims. He was just walking down the street when he was killed by a stray bullet.

PRACTICE

Answers to the following questions are given at the end of this lesson.

1. Which of the following sources for the statistic would you find most credible, and why?

   a. The National Coalition for Gun Control
   b. The FBI Crimes Division
   c. The National Rifle Association

2. Here's another example. As you read this brief student essay on divorce for a sociology class, keep in mind the issue of credibility. How would you assess the credibility of this argument? Why?

According to the U.S. Census Bureau, the divorce rate in the United States has skyrocketed in the last century. In 1900, there were approximately .6 divorces per thousand persons in the country. In 1980, the year in which divorce rates were highest, there were approximately 5.2 divorces per thousand persons. While the rate of divorce has slowed somewhat (the latest Census figures show the 1994 rate of divorce to be approximately 4.75 per thousand persons), the dramatic increases in this century demand examining. What has caused couples in this country to turn so frequently to divorce? Why is it that America, the Census Bureau informs us, has the highest divorce rate in the world?

One reason is clear. My mother, herself divorced three times, will be the first to admit it: Divorce rates have skyrocketed because it's increasingly easy to get a divorce. Because it's so easy, many couples opt for the divorce rather than trying to work out their difficulties.

Another important factor is that Americans—especially young Americans—believe in marrying for love. In fact, a survey conducted by Robert Levine,

reported in *American Demographics*, shows that of eight major countries, college students in the U.S. are least likely to marry without romantic love (just 4% compared to 51% in Pakistan). You might think that would make us more careful about whom we marry and therefore less likely to be divorced. But marriage is about more than romantic love; it's also about hard work, sacrifice, and commitment. But because American society places such a high value on romantic love (just look at the movies in the theaters and the shows on television), many couples are ready to call it quits as soon as the passion starts to fade. They don't consider that love can still be just as strong even if your spouse doesn't make your heart pound the way he or she used to. That's what I learned from my marriage. My husband and I have been together for six years now. We nearly got divorced after two years when things started to get difficult and the romance started to fade. Fortunately, we decided to try to work things out. We may still be struggling, but at least we're still together.

These two factors—the ease with which we can get a divorce and our culture's emphasis on romantic love—are to blame for sky-high divorce rates in our country. To encourage couples to stick it out, we should make it more difficult to get a divorce. And to help ease the disillusionment couples often feel when the romance starts to fade, we should produce more realistic movies and television shows and glorify mature love, not just romantic love.

IS THE EVIDENCE REASONABLE?

Now that you've considered the credibility of the arguer and the evidence she offers, the next question you should ask is whether or not the evidence is *reasonable*. This question relates mostly to evidence in the form of opinions and tentative truths.

Remember that **reasonable** means *logical*: according to conclusions drawn from evidence or from good common sense. So whenever evidence comes in the form of an opinion or tentative truth, you need to consider how reasonable that premise is. Take a look at this opinion:

If we didn't have so many guns on the street, people wouldn't be able to kill other people so easily.

Does this seem like a reasonable opinion to you? Why or why not?

However you feel about gun control, there *is* some sense to this opinion. After all, if people use guns to kill people, it seems logical that if the number of guns on the street were reduced, there would be fewer deaths. Common sense, right?

But this opinion isn't a conclusion drawn *from evidence*. Look how much stronger this premise would be if it added *evidence* to *common sense*:

If we didn't have so many guns on the street, people wouldn't be able to kill other people so easily. Take Cincinnati, for example. Strict gun control laws were put into effect in 1994, and as a result, the number of deaths by guns dropped from 1,500 in 1993 to just 600 by 1997. That's a drop of over 60%!

Notice that this statistic is used to support the opinion, which is then used to support the conclusion. In other words, this premise is part of a chain of support.

Opinions, then, can be reasonable either because they're based on good common sense or because they're drawn from evidence, like the Cincinnati example. Of course, if an opinion is reasonable on *both* accounts, it's that much stronger as support for the conclusion.

A WORD ABOUT COMMON SENSE

Before going any further, let's pause for a moment to define **common sense**. Common sense is the ability to use your general knowledge and experience to determine the best course of action in a particular situation. That includes determining whether or not to accept a claim or argument.

When you accept the opinion "If we didn't have so many guns on the street, people wouldn't be able to kill other people so easily," what you're really saying is this: In my past experience and in our general knowledge of the world, I have seen that when X is readily available, more people tend to get a hold of X; and when they have X, they're able to use it. Thus, if X weren't readily available, common sense tells us, fewer people would have X, and therefore fewer people would use X.

On the other hand, sometimes common sense isn't all that "common." Indeed, common sense often tells us things that are simply not borne out by credible, reasonable evidence. And one person's "common sense" could be another person's "ludicrous claim." Be wary when an arguer starts off by saying, "Common sense should tell you that. . . ." Some solid evidence would be more convincing!

> **Common sense**: the ability to use one's general knowledge and one's experience to determine the best course of action in a particular situation.

PRACTICE

Read statements 3–6 carefully. Are the opinions offered in the passages reasonable? If so, is the reasonableness based on common sense, or on evidence? Answers are given at the end of this lesson.

3. You should quit smoking. The smoke in your lungs can't be good for you.

4. You should quit smoking. The Surgeon General says that it causes lung cancer, emphysema, and shortness of breath.

5. Don't listen to him. He's a jerk.

6. Don't listen to him. He gave me the same advice and it almost got me fired.

7. Look again at the argument from Lesson 6 below. Are the premises in this argument reasonable? Why or why not?

He's rich, so he must be happy. All rich people are happy.

8. For a final practice exercise, evaluate the reasonableness of the argument in the essay about divorce in the United States. In this essay, the writer offers two main premises to explain why divorce rates are so high: because divorces are easy to get and because American culture places too much emphasis on romantic love. Evaluate the reasonableness of those premises. The essay is reprinted below. Write your answer in the space that follows.

According to the U.S. Census Bureau, the divorce rate in the United States has skyrocketed in the last century. In 1900, there were approximately .6 divorces per thousand persons in the country. In 1980, the year in which divorce rates were highest, there were approximately 5.2 divorces per thousand persons. While the rate of divorce has slowed somewhat (the latest Census figures show the 1994 rate of divorce to be approximately 4.75 per thousand persons), the dramatic increases in this century demand examining. What has caused couples in this country to turn so frequently to divorce? Why is it that America, the Census Bureau informs us, has the highest divorce rate in the world?

One reason is clear. My mother, herself divorced three times, will be the first to admit it: Divorce rates have skyrocketed because it's increasingly easy to get a divorce. Because it's so easy, many couples opt for the divorce rather than trying to work out their difficulties.

Another important factor is that Americans—especially young Americans—believe in marrying for love. In fact, a survey conducted by Robert Levine, reported in *American Demographics*, shows that of eight major countries, college students in the U.S. are least likely to marry without romantic love (just 4% compared to 51% in Pakistan). You might think that would make us more careful about whom we marry and therefore less likely to be divorced. But marriage is about more than romantic love; it's also about hard work, sacrifice, and commitment. But because American society places such a high value on romantic love (just look at the movies in the theaters and the shows on television), many couples are ready to call it quits as soon as the passion starts to fade. They don't consider that love can still be just as strong even if your spouse doesn't make your heart pound the way he or she used to. That's what I learned from my marriage. My husband and I have been together for six years now. We nearly got divorced after two years when things started to get difficult and the romance started to fade. Fortunately, we decided to try to work things out. We may still be struggling, but at least we're still together.

These two factors—the ease with which we can get a divorce and our culture's emphasis on romantic love—are to blame for sky-high divorce rates in our country. To encourage couples to stick it out, we should make it more difficult to get a divorce. And to help ease the disillusionment couples often feel when the romance starts to fade, we should produce more realistic movies and television shows and glorify mature love, not just romantic love.

IN SHORT

Premises can come in many forms, from statistics to feelings and opinions. When evaluating evidence, it's necessary to check for credibility and reasonableness: the credibility of the arguer, the credibility of any sources, and the reasonableness of each premise.

Skill Building Until Next Time

- As you hear deductive arguments throughout the day, pay attention to what type of evidence is offered in support of the conclusion. Statistics? Experiences? Opinions?
- Consider the credibility of the people who present you with deductive arguments today. Could they be biased? What is their level of expertise? If they offer other sources to support their arguments, are those sources credible?

ANSWERS

1. The most credible source is **b,** the FBI. Of the three possibilities, the FBI is by far the least biased. The National Coalition for Gun Control clearly has a position on gun control (for it), as does the NRA (vehemently against it).

2. This arguer (and argument) gets high marks for credibility. First, the arguer is experienced in the subject matter: she nearly went through a divorce herself and has watched her mother go through three of them. It should make you comfortable that she understands some of the factors that lead couples to divorce and that she understands how it can happen quickly and repeatedly. Second, her sources are very credible. She cites statistics from the U.S. Census Bureau, a reliable government agency, and from Robert Levine, a researcher whose work is published in a reputable, unbiased journal, *American Demographics.*

3. Reasonable, based on common sense.

4. Reasonable, based on evidence, in this case, on expert opinion.

5. Unreasonable, because the premise that follows doesn't provide a logical reason for supporting that opinion.

6. Reasonable, based on evidence—in this case, on experience.

7. No, the premises in this argument are not reasonable, and therefore the conclusion is not reasonable, either. Why not? Because good common sense should tell you that you can't make big generalizations like "All rich people are happy." You should beware of any premise that makes a claim about *all* or *none.* There is almost always an exception.

8. These premises are indeed reasonable. First, the conclusions are based on evidence:

- The Census Bureau statistics
- The Levine study
- Her mother's experience
- Her own experience

Second, they make good common sense:

- The easier it is for people to do X, the more likely it is that they will do X
- If X is portrayed often in movies and television, many people will expect reality to be the same
- People's feelings about X may change when X is no longer new

L·E·S·S·O·N

RECOGNIZING A GOOD ARGUMENT

LESSON SUMMARY

There are many components of a *good* argument—one that is convincing for good reason. This lesson will show you how to recognize and make a good deductive argument.

You got laid off from your job two months ago. You've been looking for another job but haven't had much luck. But the company you interviewed with yesterday just made you an offer. The pay isn't so good, but you're thinking about taking the job anyway; you need the money. Your friend, however, tells you not to take it: "The pay is lousy, the hours are terrible, and there are no benefits," he says. "Don't do it." Should you listen to your friend? Has he made a good argument? How can you tell?

You know what a deductive argument is. You know how to separate the conclusion from the evidence. And you know how to evaluate the evidence. These are essential steps in analyzing a deductive argument. But in order to determine the overall strength of an argument, there are several other criteria to take into consideration. Specifically, in a good deductive argument:

- The conclusion and premises are clear and complete.
- The conclusion and premises are free of excessive subtle persuasion.

- The premises are credible and reasonable.
- The premises are sufficient and substantive.
- The argument considers the other side.

You should already be familiar with the first three criteria, so we'll just take a moment to review them before we address the last two.

CLEAR AND COMPLETE

In Lesson 7, "Partial Claims and Half-Truths," you learned how to recognize incomplete claims and hidden agendas. In order for a deductive argument to hold weight, its conclusion must be clear and complete; there should be no doubt about the claim being made. The same goes for the premises; if a comparison isn't fair, or if what is being compared isn't clear, that claim cannot be valid. Evidence can't be reasonable if it is incomplete.

FREE OF EXCESSIVE SUBTLE PERSUASION

In Lesson 5, "What's In a Word?" you learned about euphemisms, dysphemisms, and biased questions. These subtle persuasion techniques are indeed manipulative, but they're not the ultimate sin when it comes to arguments. It's natural for people to choose words that will have a certain impact on their listeners. It's perfectly legitimate, for example, for someone to use a phrase like "chronic criminals" instead of "repeat offenders" if he is trying to convince you that you should support three-strikes legislation. In other words, *occasional* euphemisms, dysphemisms, and *mild* biased questions can be forgiven, and can work to the argu-

ment's advantage. But if an argument is loaded with these persuasive techniques, you should be alarmed. Generally, arguments that are heavy with euphemisms, dysphemisms, and biased questions are this way because they lack reasonable and credible evidence. In other words, the arguer may be trying to persuade you with language rather than reason because he or she lacks evidence. Excessive use of subtle persuasion also indicates that the arguer is biased about the issue.

CREDIBLE AND REASONABLE PREMISES

As discussed in the previous lesson, the two criteria for good evidence are *credibility* and *reasonableness*. Evidence is credible when it is free of bias and when the sources have a respectable level of expertise. Evidence is reasonable when it is logical, drawn from evidence or good common sense.

SUFFICIENT AND SUBSTANTIVE PREMISES

In your History of the Modern World class, you've been asked to consider whether the U.S. should have dropped the world's first atomic bomb on Hiroshima in World War II. As you think about the issue, you decide to ask your roommate, who's majoring in history, what he thinks. He says, "No, we shouldn't have dropped the bomb. It wasn't necessary."

The conclusion "we shouldn't have dropped the bomb" is clear and complete. The premise that supports the conclusion, "It wasn't necessary," is also clear and complete. The premise and conclusion are free from excessive subtle persuasion. The premise is reasonable, and you don't have any reason to doubt his credibility—

after all, he's a history major. But is this a good argument? The answer is a definite *no,* especially not for an issue of such magnitude.

Though all of the other criteria for a good argument check out, this argument has very important weakness: it simply doesn't offer enough evidence. That is, the arguer doesn't give you enough reasons to accept the conclusion. He says "it wasn't necessary," but he doesn't tell you *why.* When there is so much controversy about whether or not the U.S. should have dropped the bomb, whether it was, in fact, necessary to end the war, simply saying "it wasn't necessary" is not enough.

Here's a much better argument. What makes it better is the number of reasonable premises offered to support the conclusion. Some premises are separate support, and some are offered to support other premises (chain of support).

We shouldn't have dropped the bomb on Hiroshima. First of all, the bomb wasn't necessary to end the war. Emperor Hirohito of Japan was ready to surrender, and the Russian army was ready to invade Japan, which would have effectively ended the war.

Second, the bomb was dropped for political, not military, reasons. The government had already invested so much money in the Manhattan Project that it felt the bomb *had* to be tested somewhere, somehow. The U.S. Government also wanted to show its might by being the first country to drop such an awesome weapon of destruction. In particular, the U.S. wanted to show its supremacy over Russia, which is why the bomb was dropped before Russia invaded Japan. This way, the U.S. won the war, not the Soviet Union.

Furthermore, we shouldn't have dropped the bomb because it killed hundreds of thousands of innocent people. Hiroshima was not a military base;

most of the citizens of the city were innocent civilians who died, instantaneously or in the long agony of radiation sickness, for no good military reason.

Now you have some real reasons to accept your roommate's conclusion, don't you? What's good about this argument is not only that it offers several distinct premises that separately support the conclusion (**major premises**), but it also offers specific support (**minor premises**) for each of those major premises. In other words, each major premise is followed by one or more premises to support it. Here's how this argument maps out:

Conclusion:	We shouldn't have dropped the bomb.
Major premise:	It wasn't necessary to end the war.
Minor premise:	Japan was ready to surrender.
Minor premise:	Russia was ready to invade Japan.
Major premise:	The bomb was dropped for political, not military, reasons.
Minor premise:	The U.S. invested so much money in developing the bomb.
Minor premise:	The U.S. government wanted to show its might by being the first to drop the bomb.
Minor premise:	The U.S. wanted to show its supremacy over Russia.
Major premise:	It killed hundreds of thousands of innocent people.
Minor premise:	Hiroshima was not a military base.
Minor premise:	Most of the citizens were innocent civilians.

PRACTICE

1. Take the following argument and make it substantial. Provide more evidence by adding major and minor supporting premises. A sample answer is given at the end of this lesson.

Public school students should wear uniforms just like private school students do. Uniforms will create a stronger sense of community.

Stronger argument:

CONSIDERING THE OTHER SIDE

At the beginning of this lesson, your friend tried to talk you out of taking that job offer. Did he provide a good argument based on the criteria we've discussed so far? Here's his argument again to refresh your memory:

"The pay is lousy, the hours are terrible, and there are no benefits," he says. "Don't do it."

Well, his argument is reasonable, credible, free of subtle persuasion, and he offers three different reasons, though they could be supported with specific details (minor premises). Still, this argument lacks one criterion of a good argument; it does not consider counter-arguments.

Counter-arguments are those arguments that might be offered by someone arguing for the other side. That is, if you are arguing that it's better to live in the city than in the country, you need to keep in mind what someone arguing that living in the country is better than living in the city might think. By considering counter-arguments, you show your critical thinking skills—whatever your opinion, you have considered all sides of the issue. And this helps demonstrate your credibility, too; it shows that you've done your homework, that you know something about the issue and that you've thought carefully about the logic of your position.

For example, when you hear your friend's argument, what thoughts might go through your mind? You might have been thinking about the following reasons to *take* the job rather than reject it:

- You really need the money.
- You can advance quickly.
- You'll have benefits after 6 months.
- You can switch to a different shift after 6 months.
- It's a lot closer to your home than your previous job.

If your friend really wants to convince you not to take the job, he'll not only support his conclusion with credible, reasonable, and ample evidence, he'll also show that he knows why you might want to say yes—and why his reasons for saying no are better.

One way to help you develop a better argument is to play devil's advocate. When you're getting ready to make an argument, write down your conclusion and your premises, and then do the same for the *opposite* position. Pretend that you are in court and you are both the prosecution and the defense. This will help you anticipate what the other side will say so you can come up with premises to *counter* their argument. Look how much stronger your friend's argument is when he considers the other side:

> Don't take that job. I know you really need the money, but the pay is lousy. It's a full three dollars less per hour than your last job. You can probably move through the ranks quickly, but because you'd be starting at a lower pay scale, you'd have to take several steps just to get back up to your old salary. And you have to wait six months before you can switch shifts and get benefits. What if something happens in the meantime? True, you'll save time and gas because it's closer, but is that extra thirty minutes a day worth it?

Notice two things that your friend does here. First, he systematically and carefully acknowledges each of your concerns. Second, he counters each of those concerns with a reasonable premise supporting his point of view. Furthermore, he improved his argument by adding specific minor premises, like the fact that the pay is three dollars less per hour.

Because addressing counterarguments is so crucial to making a good argument, let's look at another example. You've heard your roommate's position on the bombing of Hiroshima, and you think you agree, but to be sure, you decide to play devil's advocate so that you can address counterarguments and refute or downplay them in your essay. Here are the premises you might come up with to support the conclusion that the U.S. *should* have dropped the bomb:

Conclusion: While it may not have been necessary to end the war, the bomb-

ing of Hiroshima was necessary to save thousands of American lives and to establish the United States as the leading world superpower.

Major premise: Had the Enola Gay not dropped the world's first atomic bomb on Hiroshima early that August morning, forcing Japan to surrender a few days later, thousands of American troops would have been lost.

Minor premises: American troops were scheduled to invaded Japan within a few months. Because of the kamikaze mentality of both Japanese troops and civilians, American casualties would have been extremely high.

Major premise: Furthermore, dropping the bomb was the first step in winning the war against Communism.

Minor premises: Dropping the bomb before the Soviet Union invaded Japan established the supremacy of the U.S. military and its firepower. This illustrated the challenge that the Soviet Union would face as it tried to spread Communism throughout Europe.

Major premise: In addition, the bomb established the scientific and technological supremacy of the United States.

Minor premise: Several countries around the globe were working on an atomic weapon, but the U.S. was able to develop the bomb faster and more efficiently.

Now you can build a good, strong argument that addresses these issues. For example, you might write:

While the dropping of the bomb did establish the scientific and technological supremacy of the United States, it did not have to be dropped on a city—taking the lives of thousands of innocent men, women, and children—to demonstrate its destructive power.

PRACTICE

A version of the school uniform argument is printed below. Play devil's advocate and make a list of counter-arguments. Then rewrite the argument to make it stronger.

Public school students should wear uniforms just like private school students do. For one thing, **uniforms will create a stronger sense of community**. It's important for children to feel like they belong, and uniforms are a powerful physical and psychological way to create that sense of belonging. **Uniforms also improve discipline**. According to the Department of Education, private schools across the country have fewer discipline problems than public schools, and the handful of public schools that have experimented with uniforms have found their discipline problems decreased sharply. Furthermore, **uniforms**

can help increase the self-esteem of children from poorer families. If everyone wears the same clothes, they don't have to come to school ashamed of their hand-me-downs or second-hand clothing.

2. **Counter-arguments:**

3. **Revised argument:**

IN SHORT

Good deductive arguments meet the following criteria:

- The conclusion and premises are clear and complete.
- The conclusion and premises are free of excessive subtle persuasion.
- The premises are credible and reasonable.
- The premises are sufficient and substantive.
- The argument considers the other side.

The more of these criteria your arguments meet, the more convincing you'll be.

> ### Skill Building Until Next Time
>
> - Practice building your argument skills by playing devil's advocate. When you hear a deductive argument, think about what someone taking the opposite position might argue.
> - When you hear or make an argument today, try to add more support to that argument. Add another major premise or add minor premises to support the major premises.

ANSWERS

1. Answers will vary depending upon what premises you chose to support this argument. At any rate, your argument should be significantly longer than the first version. Here's one revision that provides several major and minor premises to support the conclusion. The major premises are highlighted.

Public school students should wear uniforms just like private school students do. For one thing, **uniforms will create a stronger sense of community**. It's important for children to feel like they belong, and uniforms are a powerful physical and psychological way to create that sense of belonging. **Uniforms also improve discipline**. According to the Department of Education, private schools across the country have fewer discipline problems than public schools, and the handful of public schools that have experimented with uniforms have found their discipline problems decreased sharply. Furthermore, **uniforms can help increase the self-esteem of children from poorer families**. If everyone wears the same clothes, they don't have to come to school ashamed of their hand-me-downs or second-hand clothing.

2. Your counter-arguments might look something like the following:
   a. Uniforms won't create a stronger sense of community; they'll create a culture of conformity.
   b. Uniforms alone won't decrease discipline problems. The problem goes too deep.
   c. Students from poorer families will still have cheaper shoes, coats, etc. Uniforms can't hide their socioeconomic status.

3. Your revised argument, of course, depends upon your counter-arguments. Here's how the above counter-arguments might be incorporated. The sentences that address counter-arguments are boldfaced.

Public school students should wear uniforms just like private school students do. For one thing, uniforms will create a stronger sense of community. It's important for children to feel like they belong, and uniforms are a powerful physical and psychological way to create that sense of belonging. **While some worry that uniforms encourage conformity, a sense of belonging helps give students the self-esteem**

they need to be themselves. Uniforms also improve discipline. According to the Department of Education, private schools across the country have fewer discipline problems than public schools, and the handful of public schools that have experimented with uniforms have found their discipline problems decreased sharply. **This demonstrates that uniforms alone can have a profound affect on discipline.** Furthermore, uniforms can help increase the self-esteem of children from poorer families. If everyone wears the same clothes, they don't have to come to school ashamed of their hand-me-downs or second-hand clothing. **Though uniforms won't alleviate their poverty, and though they still won't be able to afford the kinds of shoes and accessories that wealthier children sport, uniforms *will* enable them to feel significantly more comfortable among their peers.**

L·E·S·S·O·N
PUTTING IT ALL TOGETHER

LESSON SUMMARY

This lesson puts together the strategies and skills you learned in Lessons 1–9. You'll review the key points of each lesson and practice evaluating claims and arguments.

Before going any further, it's time to review all of what you've learned in the preceding lessons so that you can combine strategies and put them to practical use. Repetition will help solidify ideas about what makes a good argument in your memory. Let's go through each lesson one at a time.

LESSON 1: CRITICAL THINKING AND REASONING SKILLS

You learned that critical thinking means carefully considering a problem, claim, question, or situation in order to determine the best solution. You also learned that reasoning skills involve using good sense and basing our reasons for doing things in facts, evidence, or logical conclusions. Finally, you learned that critical thinking and reasoning skills will help you compose strong arguments, assess the validity of other people's arguments, make more effective and logical decisions, and solve problems and puzzles more efficiently and effectively.

LESSON 2: PROBLEM SOLVING STRATEGIES

You learned that the first step in solving any problem is to clearly identify the main issue and then break the problem down into its various parts. Next, you need to prioritize the issues and make sure that they're all relevant.

LESSON 3: THINKING VS. KNOWING

You practiced distinguishing between fact and opinion. Facts are things *known* for certain to have happened, to be true, or to exist. Opinions are things *believed* to have happened, to be true, or to exist. Tentative truths are claims that are thought to be facts but that are not verifiable.

LESSON 4: WHO MAKES THE CLAIM?

You learned how to evaluate the credibility of a claim by learning how to measure reliability, how to recognize bias, and how to determine the level of expertise of a source. You also learned why eyewitnesses aren't always credible.

LESSON 5: WHAT'S IN A WORD?

You learned how euphemisms, dysphemisms, and biased questions can be used to get people to react in a certain way. Euphemisms replace negative expressions with positive ones; dysphemisms replace neutral or positive expressions with negative ones; and biased questions make it difficult for you to answer questions fairly.

LESSON 6: WORKING WITH ARGUMENTS

You learned that deductive arguments move from a conclusion to supporting premises. You practiced identifying the conclusion and learned the difference between premises that provide separate support and those that are part of a chain of support.

LESSON 7: PARTIAL CLAIMS AND HALF-TRUTHS

You practiced identifying incomplete claims like those that often appear in advertisements. You also learned the different types of averages and how the word "averages" can be misleading.

LESSON 8: EVALUATING EVIDENCE

You practiced looking carefully at evidence to determine whether or not it is valid. The two key criteria you looked for were credibility and reasonableness.

LESSON 9: RECOGNIZING A GOOD ARGUMENT

Finally, you learned what makes a good argument: a conclusion and premises that are clear, complete, and free of excessive subtle persuasion; premises that are credible, reasonable, sufficient, and substantive; and consideration of counterarguments.

If any of these terms or strategies sound unfamiliar to you, STOP. Take a few minutes to review whatever lesson is unclear.

Now it's time for you to practice. Answers are given at the end of this lesson.

PRACTICE

You are on a crowded bus headed downtown. A burly, angry-looking man has just demanded that you give up your seat for him.

1. What is the main problem or issue?

2. What are the parts of the problem?

3. Consider the priority of these issues. What part of the problem should you address first? Second?

Below is a brief deductive argument. Read it carefully and then answer the questions that follow. The sentences are lettered to make the answers easier to follow.

(a) Basketball players can earn millions in just one season. (b) Football players can earn hundreds of thousands for just a 30-second commercial. (c) Meanwhile, a teacher can't earn more than $50,000 a year doing one of the toughest jobs in the world. (d) These saints work a lot harder and deserve to get paid a lot more for the miracles they perform on a daily basis. (e) Who is more important—the woman who taught you how to read and write so that you can succeed in life, or the jock who plays for a living? (f) The average salary for professional athletes is $650,000. (g) That's more than ten times what the average public high school principal makes. (h) It's a disgrace that even benchwarmers make more in a month than I do all year.

4. Underline any opinions you find in this passage.

5. Put brackets [ ] around any claims that you feel are tentative truths.

6. Are there any incomplete claims in this argument?

7. Evaluate the use of the word *average* in this passage. Is it acceptable?

8. Highlight any euphemisms, dysphemisms, or biased questions.

9. What is the conclusion of this argument?

10. What are the premises that support that conclusion?

11. Evaluate those premises. Are they credible? Reasonable?

12. Would you say that this is a good argument? Why or why not?

13. Rewrite this argument to make it stronger. With you as author, you should be able to remove the issue of author bias. For the sake of this exercise, make up sources that would give your facts more credibility. Also, be sure to address counterarguments.

Skill Building Until Next Time

- Review the "Skill Building" sections from each lesson in the past two weeks. Try any that you didn't do.
- Imagine you've been sent to this class by your employer and that in return for free tuition, you must share what you learn with your colleagues. Write a detailed memo to your colleagues explaining what you've learned in the last ten lessons.

ANSWERS

1. The main problem is deciding whether or not to give him your seat.

2. There are several issues here, including the following:

   - Could you be in danger if you refuse?
   - Will you be embarrassed if you give him your seat?
   - How should you tell him *no* if you decide to refuse?
   - Will others around you come to your aid if you refuse and he gets violent?
   - Are there any open seats on the bus? If so, then he may be looking for a fight.
   - How soon will you be getting off the bus?
   - Could he be ill? How can you tell?
   - How are you feeling? Do you need to sit down?
   - Do you notice anything about him to suggest that he may be violent?

3. The first issue you should probably address is your safety. In order to assess whether or not you are in danger if you refuse, there are other issues you'll have to address, including whether or not it appears that he's looking for a fight and whether or not you notice any signs that he may

be violent. After you assess the level of danger, then you can consider other factors. If, for example, it looks like a refusal will result in trouble, are there other seats you could move to? Can you simply get off the bus at the next stop?

4, 5, and **8.** Opinions are underlined, tentative truths are bracketed, and persuasive techniques are highlighted below:

[Basketball players can earn millions in just one season. Football players can earn hundreds of thousands for just a 30-second commercial. Meanwhile, a teacher can't earn more than $50,000 a year] doing <u>one of the toughest jobs in the world</u>. <u>These **saints** work a lot harder and deserve to get paid a lot more for the **miracles** they perform on a daily basis</u>. **Who is more important—the woman who taught you how to read and write so that you can succeed in life, or the jock who plays for a living?** [The average salary for professional athletes is $650,000.] [That's more than ten times what the average public high school principal makes.] <u>It's a disgrace that [even **benchwarmers** make more in a month than I do all year.]</u>

6. Yes. The arguer claims that "These saints work a lot harder and deserve to get paid a lot more…." Harder than what? More than what? The implied comparison is to professional athletes, but notice that the claim itself doesn't make that connection.

7. Yes and no. The first average salary, given in sentence **f,** for professional athletes, is troublesome for several reasons. There are many professional sports—professional volleyball, for example, or table tennis—where the salaries for even the top players don't approach $650,000. If you were to survey all professional athletes, you'd probably find that the typical player doesn't come close to a six-figure salary. However, because there are players like Michael Jordan and Dion Sanders, whose salaries are in the millions, the *average* is higher than the typical. The second average, given in sentence **g,** however, is more acceptable. There isn't likely to be such a drastic range in public school principal salaries.

9. The conclusion is the fourth sentence: "These saints work a lot harder and deserve to get paid a lot more for the miracles they perform on a daily basis."

10. The premises that support this conclusion include sentences **a, b, c, f, g,** and **h.** Sentence **d** is the conclusion, and sentence **e** can't be a claim since it is a question.

11. The whole argument must be called into question when the credibility of the arguer is considered. The last sentence states that the arguer is a teacher himself, which clearly indicates a bias. On the other hand, it does suggest that he has some expertise in the realm of teacher salary and how hard teachers work. But because the argument fails to provide sources for its figures, they can't be accepted as facts, and that weakens their credibility. If those figures could be verified, then the premises are reasonable. Furthermore, the premise in the last sentence can't be accepted because no figures are given to prove it valid. In addition, there's the very strong possibility that benchwarmers in sports like table tennis don't make much at all.

12. Overall this is a poor argument. As much as anyone may believe that teachers deserve to be paid more than they earn, or that some professional athletes are grossly overpaid, the argument is not very effective. Why not? The first problem is that the conclusion is not complete. Second, there's quite a bit of subtle persuasion in this argument. Third, there are problems with the credibility of the arguer and his sources. Fourth, the argument fails to consider counter-arguments.

13. Answers will vary. Here is one possibility:

Basketball players can earn millions in just one season. Michael Jordan, for example, earns over $24 million a year playing for the Bulls and over $50 million in endorsements. Football players can earn hundreds of thousands for a 30-second commercial. Dion Sanders, for example, was paid $900,000 just to take a bite out of a Big Mac. Meanwhile, a teacher with 15 years' experience earns little more than $40,000 a year—the mean salary for a teacher with 15 years' experience, according to the Department of Education—doing one of the toughest jobs in the world. True, professional athletes provide entertainment and serve as role models for many children, but teachers perform a much more important service on a daily basis by providing children with the tools they need to succeed in life.

Some will argue that players deserve such high salaries because they risk permanent physical injury—even possible death—every day they play the sport. Furthermore, they have a limited career—most athletes must give up the sport long before they reach age the age of 40. These are valid arguments; however, as schools become increasingly violent, it's important to note that teachers now have a job that puts them at risk. Furthermore, the extreme seven and eight figure salaries of professional athletes far exceed what they need for an early retirement.

The mean salary of a professional basketball player, according to the NBA, is $650,000 a year. That's ten times the mean salary for public high school principles in New York City. It's a sad statement about our society that even athletes who spend most of the game on the bench make more in a year than Mrs. McMurphy, the woman who taught me my ABC's.

L · E · S · S · O · N

LOGICAL FALLACIES: APPEALS TO EMOTION

LESSON SUMMARY

Arguments that appeal to people's emotions rather than their sense of logic and reason abound in everyday life. In this lesson, you'll learn how to recognize several common appeals to emotion so that you can make more informed and logical decisions.

ou're 28 years old and the proud father of a one-year-old girl. As you rock her to sleep one night, you hear the following commercial on the radio:

Do you have a child who was born within the last year? Did you know that by the time your child is ready for college, the average college tuition will cost over $100,000 a year? Don't make a mistake that your child will pay for for the rest of her life. Make sure you have enough money to pay for your child's college education. Invest with Tuition-Care today. Call 1-800-TUITION.

The next morning, you're on the phone with Tuition-Care. Why? How did they get your business?

It's probably not hard to see that Tuition-Care took advantage of your desire to provide for your child—and your fear that you may not be able to afford her college tuition. But notice that Tuition-Care didn't provide you with any logical reasons to invest with them. Instead, they got your business by manipulating your emotions.

There are many strategies people will use to try to convince you that their conclusions are sound. Unfortunately, many of these strategies *appear* to be logical when, in fact, they're not. These strategies—often called **logical fallacies** or **pseudoreasoning** (false reasoning)—can lead you to make poor decisions and accept arguments that really don't hold water. That's why the next three lessons go over some of the most common logical fallacies. The more of them you can recognize—and the more you can avoid them in your own arguments—the better problem-solver and decision-maker you will be.

This lesson deals with four fallacies that appeal to your emotions rather than your sense of reason: scare tactics, flattery, peer pressure, and appeals to pity.

SCARE TACTICS

In the opening scenario, Tuition-Care appealed to your sense of fear. You decided to invest with them because you were afraid of what might happen if you didn't. While it certainly makes sense to start saving for your daughter's tuition (and the earlier the better), that's not a logical reason to start saving with Tuition-Care. Until you learn more about how Tuition-Care works—and how it compares to other opportunities for saving for college tuition—you shouldn't invest your hard-earned money there. Tuition-Care's commercial didn't provide you with any information about its investment program. Instead, Tuition-Care played upon your emotions, using a logical fallacy often called scare tactics.

Scare tactics are used very commonly in deductive arguments, and they can be quite powerful. Note that scare tactics are different from warnings. Warnings are claims about real threats to your physical or emotional well being, like "you better not touch that pan." Though the premises are often left unstated, warnings are based in good reasoning ("It's very hot and you'll burn your hand"). Scare tactics, on the other hand, are attempts to "scare" you into accepting a claim without offering you good, reasonable evidence. Once you know what to look for, scare tactics are pretty easy to recognize. For example, read the following argument:

Support gun control—or you could be next.

Sounds convincing, doesn't it? After all, who wants to be the next victim? But is this a good argument? Notice that the only reason this argument gives you for supporting the conclusion is emotional. It aims to *frighten* you into supporting gun control. The argument would be much more powerful if it also provided a logical reason for your support.

PRACTICE

Read the following arguments carefully. If the argument uses logic to support the conclusion, write an L in the blank. If the argument uses scare tactics, write an S in the blank. You'll find the answers at the end of this lesson.

_____ **1.** I know I'm not due for a raise yet, Ms. Trible, but I thought you might consider an early increase, especially since you don't want the other employees to find out about the large pay increase you gave yourself last year.

_____ **2.** You can type this paper for me, can't you, Ray? That way I won't have to tell Carla you were out with Marie last night.

_____ **3.** Hand in your paper on time or you will fail the class.

FLATTERY

They say flattery will get you nowhere, but they're wrong. Flattery is powerful—so powerful, in fact, that it often leads people to make poor decisions and to accept arguments that really have no logical basis. Just as people can appeal to the sense of fear, they can also appeal to our **vanity,** which is another logical fallacy. Here's an example:

You're a good citizen. You care about the future. That's why we know we can count on you to re-elect Senator Houseman.

Notice how this argument doesn't give you any logical reasons for re-electing Senator Houseman. Instead, it flatters you; you like hearing that you're a good citizen and someone who cares about the future. While this may be true about you, is that any reason to re-elect the senator? Not without evidence that he's done a good job in his first term. This argument doesn't give any evidence of his job performance.

Here's another example of an appeal to vanity:

"Professor Wilkins, this is the best class I've ever taken. I'm learning so much from you! Thank you. By the way, I know that I missed an exam last week and that you normally don't let students make up missed exams. However, since you are such an understanding teacher, I thought you'd allow me to make up the test."

Here, the student doesn't give the teacher any reason to make an exception to her no-make-up policy. She may indeed be an excellent teacher and the student may indeed be learning a lot from her, but he's not giving her any good reasons; he's just buttering her up to get her to say yes. He could add logic to his flattery by also telling her he had been in the hospital, or at a funeral, or attending some sort of emergency. But as it stands, it's just plain flattery.

PRACTICE

Read the following arguments carefully. Are they using logic (L) or appealing to vanity (V)? You'll find the answers at the end of this lesson.

_____ **4.** Teacher to class: "Thank you all for a wonderful semester. I've really enjoyed this class—you're quite a talented group of students. Now, I have these end-of-the-semester evaluations I need you to fill out. I know you'll all be honest and fill them out carefully."

_____ **5.** "Claire, I'd like you to handle this typing project. You're the fastest typist and the best at reading my handwriting."

_____ **6.** "Claire, I know you don't mind a little extra work—you're such a good sport! So I'd like you to handle this typing project. You're the best."

PEER PRESSURE

Along with fear and vanity, another extremely powerful emotion is our desire to be accepted by others. As children, people often do things they know are wrong because of pressure from friends. Unfortunately, many people continue to give in to peer pressure throughout their lives. **Peer pressure** is another form of false reasoning. It is an argument that says, "Accept the conclusion, or *you* won't be accepted." Take a look at the following arguments for examples of peer pressure:

"Just make up the experiment results. We did."

"We're all voting *no,* Joe. You should, too."

In both of these examples, the arguers don't offer any logical reasons for accepting their conclusions. Instead, they offer you acceptance—you'll be like everyone else. It's the old "everyone else is doing it" argument. The counter-argument is exactly the one your mother gave you: If everyone else were jumping off a cliff, would you do it, too?

No one likes to be left out, and that's why we often give in to peer pressure. It *is* hard to be different and stand alone. But it is important to remember that our desire to belong is *not* a logical reason for accepting an argument. *Why* should Joe vote *no?* He needs to hear some specific, logical reasons. Otherwise, he's just falling victim to false logic.

PRACTICE

Read the following arguments carefully. Are the arguers using logic (L) or peer pressure (P) to try to convince you? You'll find the answers at the end of this lesson.

____ **7.** "*We* all think that the death penalty is the only way to cure society of rampant crime. Don't you agree?"

____ **8.** "Come on, we're all voting Democratic again, just like the last time."

____ **9.** "Stick with your party, Joe. The more unified we are, the more likely our candidates will win."

____ **10.** "Take this class with us, Pera. We all need it for our major and we could study together."

PITY

You are a student member of the Academic Affairs Committee. You are hearing the case of a student caught cheating on an exam. The penalty for students caught cheating is a one-semester suspension. "Please don't suspend me," he begs. "I'll lose all of my financial aid and I'll have to transfer to another college. And my parents will kill me!"

What should you do?
a. Expel him. You can't stand people who beg.
b. Let him go with a warning. After all, it's just one test.
c. Suspend him for one semester.

Clearly, option **a** is unreasonable. But should you give him a break because he'll lose his financial aid and get in trouble with his parents? Are these good reasons for departing from university policy?

Regardless of how badly you might feel about the consequences this student will face, **c** is the most appropriate course of action. The student tried to convince you otherwise, however, by appealing to another one of the most powerful emotions—the sense of pity and compassion for others. No one wants to be seen as heartless or uncaring. And that's why the appeal to **pity**, another logical fallacy, often works.

Here's another example of an appeal to pity:

Think of all the families of the murder victims. Think of their suffering. Think of their pain and agony. Support capital punishment—for their sake.

Notice that this argument asks the listener to support a cause purely for *emotional* reasons. It appeals to the sense of compassion for the families who lost a loved one. While this may be a compelling argument—after all, the families of the victims do deserve compassion—it is not a *logical* one. It doesn't directly address *why* capital punishment is a reasonable policy.

Of course you will have to judge each situation individually. But just as with the other appeals to emotion, it's important to have some logical reasons to balance the emotional. Because it's often difficult to determine whether or not an argument is an appeal to pity or a legitimate argument, it helps to return to something you learned back in Lesson 1: justifying your actions. Before you act, ask yourself, "Why am I doing this?" If the answer is "because I feel sorry for X," you know you're committing a logical fallacy.

Sometimes, of course, it is appropriate to act solely out of your sense of compassion for others. You might give a homeless person money or a colleague a batch of flowers for precisely that reason. But on other occasions, acting out of pity is likely to lead you to trouble.

There are some people in the world who will take advantage of your sense of compassion, so think carefully before you act on pity alone.

PRACTICE

Read the following arguments carefully. Are they using logic (L) to convince you, or are they appealing to your sense of pity and compassion (P)? You'll find the answers at the end of this lesson.

____11. "But you can't fire me, Mr. Watts. I have seven mouths to feed!"

____12. "But you can't fire me, Mr. Watts. I'm the only one who knows how to repair the machine. Besides, I have seven mouths to feed!"

____13. I know I didn't hand my paper in on time, Professor Yang. But I was in Georgia. My brother was in a terrible accident, and I spent the weekend in the hospital. I took my books with me but I just couldn't concentrate. He's still in Intensive Care. Would it be possible to hand in the paper in two weeks?

____14. I'd really like a chance to take the midterm again, Professor Ramirez. My GPA is in bad shape and I'm already failing one of my other classes.

IN SHORT

Appeals to emotions, including fear, vanity, desire to belong, and pity, can be very powerful. It is important to recognize when an argument uses emotional appeals—especially when emotional appeals are the only kind of support the argument offers.

Skill Building Until Next Time

- Be on the lookout for emotional appeals throughout the day, especially in advertisments.
- Think about something that you want someone to do for you. Think of several good, logical reasons for that person to say yes. Then, think of four different emotional appeals—one from each category—that you might use if you didn't know better.

ANSWERS

1. **S.** This argument suggests that the speaker will tell others about Ms. Trible's raise. That is not, however, a good reason to give the speaker an early raise.

2. **S.** This argument suggests that Ray should type the speaker's paper because if he doesn't, the speaker will get Ray in trouble with Carla. However, that has no bearing on the typing of the paper.

3. **L.** This is a logical reason to hand in your paper on time.

4. **V.** This is a definite appeal to the students' vanity. The teacher is hoping that by buttering the students up a bit—telling them how wonderful they are—they'll be more generous in return in their evaluations of the class.

5. **L.** The speaker provides two logical, practical reasons for Claire to handle the project.

6. **V.** The speaker is trying to convince Claire she should do the extra work by flattering her. Notice that none of the reasons directly relates to her ability to do the work well.

7. **P.** The speaker tries to get agreement by stressing that everyone else thinks that way. He suggests that if you disagree, you'll be alone in your belief.

8. **P.** Again, the speaker is using peer pressure. Here, the suggestion is that everyone else is voting the same way, so you should, too. But the speaker doesn't provide any logical reasons for voting for the Democrat.

9. **L.** This time the speaker gives Joe a good logical reason for voting along the party line: their party's candidates will win.

10. **L.** The speaker gives two good reasons for accepting the conclusion.

11. **P.** The only reason the speaker gives for not being fired is that he has a family to feed. He doesn't make any argument about his ability to perform his duties at work.

12. **L.** And a little pity. The employee offers a powerful, logical reason for not firing him as well as an emotional one.

13. **L.** If what the student says is true, this is a valid reason for giving the student extra time to finish his or her work.

14. **P.** Neither of these are valid reasons for letting the student take the exam over. Unfortunately, he or she will have to suffer the consequences.

L·E·S·S·O·N
LOGICAL FALLACIES: THE IMPOSTORS

LESSON SUMMARY

Some forms of logical fallacies are tougher to recognize than others because they *look* logical. This lesson will help you spot several common fallacies, including *circular reasoning* and *two wrongs make a right.*

Either you're with us or you're against us. Which is it?" Have you ever been put on the spot like this before, where you were forced to decide between two contradictory options? Chances are you have. But chances are you also had more choices than you thought.

Logical fallacies come in many forms. The last lesson covered the false reasoning that appeals to your emotions rather than your sense of logic. This lesson will look at four logical fallacies that are sometimes a little harder to detect because they don't appeal to your emotions. As a result, they may *look* logical even though they aren't. These types of fallacies are logical impostors. Four types will be covered in this lesson, including *no in-betweens, slippery slope, circular reasoning,* and *two wrongs make a right.*

CRITICAL THINKING AND LOGIC SKILLS

No In-Betweens

No in-betweens (also called *false dilemma*) is a logical fallacy that aims to convince you that there are only two choices: there is X and there is Y, and nothing in between. The "logic" behind this fallacy is that if you think there are only two choices, then you won't stop to consider other possibilities. The arguer hopes that you will therefore be more likely to accept his or her conclusion.

For example, imagine that you work for a small company. You're in a meeting where the topic is how to better market your product. A colleague says, "Look, either we do a full-color glossy brochure or we don't do anything at all. It's better to have nothing than to have something shabby. Do it right or don't do it at all."

While it may be tempting to agree, your colleague hasn't presented a good argument. Though he may want the top-of-the-line brochure, that doesn't mean it's top-of-the-line or nothing. The company has to start somewhere. A black and white brochure costs less and may just do the trick to start bringing in more business.

The *no in-betweens* fallacy is often used to pressure you into taking a certain position. For example, you might hear "Either you're a Republican or you're a Democrat. There's nothing in between." But there is— you could be independent (not registered with any party), you could be a member of the Independent Party, you could be a member of the Green Party, and so on. You could also be a Democrat who votes Republican on certain issues (or vice versa). In other words, there are plenty of in-betweens.

It is important to remember that there are very few situations in which there are only two options. There are almost always other choices.

Practice

Read the following arguments carefully. Do the arguers use logic (L) or no in-betweens (NI) to convince you? You'll find the answers at the end of this lesson.

_____**1.** Mother to son: "Either you major in engineering or in pre-med. Nothing else will lead to a good career."

_____**2.** If this money doesn't go right into the bank, it's going to go to waste.

_____**3.** Partner 1 of 2: "We can divide the work, or work together on the whole thing, or one of us can do it all. Which do you prefer?"

_____**4.** Either we raise taxes by 10% or we drown ourselves in a budget deficit.

_____**5.** Look, either you support abortion or you don't. You can't have it both ways.

Slippery Slope

If scientists are allowed to experiment with cloning humans, next thing you know they'll be mass producing people on assembly lines.

Right?

Well, maybe. But probably not, and definitely not necessarily. This type of logical fallacy—often called **slippery slope**—presents an if/then scenario. It argues that if X happens, then Y will follow. This "next thing you know" argument has one major flaw, however: X doesn't necessarily lead to Y. When you hear someone make a claim in this format, you need your critical thinking and reasoning skills to come into play.

96   LESSON 12 • *LearningExpress Basic Skills for College*

You need to carefully consider whether or not there's a logical relationship between X and Y.

If scientists were to experiment with cloning human beings, for example, does that *necessarily* mean that humans will be mass produced on production lines? Definitely not. First of all, it may prove impossible to clone humans. Second, if it is possible, it's a far step from a single clone to assembly-line production of clones. And third, if assembly-line cloning *is* possible, it's likely that it will be forbidden. So though the thought of mass-produced human beings is frightening, it's not logical to restrict experiments because we're afraid of consequences that aren't likely to happen. More logical reasons need to be presented to justify limiting that kind of experimentation.

PRACTICE

Read the following arguments carefully. Are they using logic (L) or slippery slope (SS) to convince you? You'll find the answers at the end of this lesson.

_____ **6.** If we legalize marijuana, watch out—the legalization of cocaine and other drugs can't be far behind.

_____ **7.** I don't think the "three strikes and you're out" policy for convicted felons is a good policy. Before you know it, it'll be two strikes, then just one.

_____ **8.** I wouldn't drop this class if I were you. If you do, you'll be three credits behind and you'll have to take an extra class next semester to graduate on time.

CIRCULAR REASONING

You're in a meeting when you decide to bring up what you think is an important issue. When you're finished, your boss turns to you and says, "Well, that's not important."

"Why not?" you ask.

"Because it just doesn't matter," he replies.

Your boss has just committed a very common logical fallacy called **circular reasoning** (also known as *begging the question*). Circular reasoning is a very appropriate name, because that's what this false logic does: it goes in a circle. Notice how your boss's argument doubles back on itself. In other words, his conclusion and premise say essentially the same thing:

Conclusion: That's not important.
Premise: It doesn't matter.

Instead of progressing logically from conclusion to evidence, the argument gets stuck at the conclusion. Like a dog chasing its tail, it goes nowhere. Here's another example:

This ad campaign is no good. It just isn't working.

Notice how the premise, "it just isn't working," is no support for the conclusion, "this ad campaign is no good." The premise simply restates the conclusion rather than providing specific evidence to support it like "we haven't gotten a single new customer." Again, the argument goes nowhere.

Circular reasoning can be particularly tricky because a conclusion that doubles back on itself often *sounds* strong. That is, by restating the conclusion, you reinforce the idea that you're trying to convey. But you're *not* offering any logical reasons to accept that argument.

When you hear someone make a claim that follows this format, look for a logical premise to support the conclusion—you probably won't find one.

PRACTICE

See if you can recognize circular reasoning in the following arguments. If the argument is logical, write an L in the blank. If the argument is circular, write a C in the blank.

_____ **9.** You should give me half of that commission, Johnson. I deserve 50%.

_____ **10.** I think his writing style is hard to understand; his language is confusing.

_____ **11.** You should take the internship because it's good experience.

_____ **12.** It's the right thing to do, Wilson. This way no one will get hurt.

_____ **13.** We believe it's the best choice because it's the right thing to do.

TWO WRONGS MAKE A RIGHT

Your friend tells you she just turned in an awful evaluation of her physics professor. "Why did you give her such a bad evaluation?" you ask. "I thought you said she was a great teacher."

"She is," your friend replies, "but she's going to give me a bad grade."

Fair's fair, right? Wrong. Your friend hasn't made a logical argument here. Instead, she's guilty of the *two wrongs make a right* fallacy.

The **two wrongs make a right** fallacy assumes that it's OK for you to do something to someone else because of what you think that someone else *might* do to you. But two wrongs *don't* make a right, especially when you're talking about *mights*. If your friend's professor *might* give her a bad grade, does that make it OK for your friend to write up a bad evaluation? Of course not. The only reason she should write a negative evaluation is if her professor is not a good teacher.

Don't get this fallacy confused with the *eye-for-an-eye* argument. The *two wrongs* logical fallacy is not about getting even. It's about getting an edge. In an eye for an eye, you do something to someone because that person has *already* done it to you. But two wrongs make a right argues that you can do something simply because someone else *might* do it to you. And that's neither logical nor fair.

To show you how illogical this fallacy is, imagine what would have happened if the United States and the former Soviet Union had taken the two wrongs make a right approach during the cold war. If they had, you probably wouldn't be here today to be going through this lesson. The U.S. government would have said, "Well, the Russians might bomb us, so let's get them first." And the Russians would have said, "The Americans might attack us, so let's bomb them instead." This approach would have ended in nuclear holocaust.

This is, of course, an exaggerated example, but you get the idea. Two wrongs that are built on a *maybe*—even a *probably*—don't make a right.

PRACTICE

14. Put a check mark next to the arguments below that use the two wrongs make a right fallacy.

  a. Go ahead, tell your boss what you saw Edgar do. You know he'd report you in a second if he ever saw you do something like that.

  b. The death penalty makes sense. People convicted of murder should be murdered themselves.

  c. The insurance company made an error in my favor! Well, I'm not going to point it out to them. They'd never let me know if they accidentally overcharged me and I paid too much.

In Short

Logical fallacies can appear to be logical; to avoid falling into their traps, you need to be on the lookout for false reasoning. The **no in-betweens** fallacy tries to convince you that there are only two choices when in reality there are many options. The **slippery slope** fallacy tries to convince you that if you do X, then Y will follow—but in reality, X doesn't necessarily lead to Y. **Circular reasoning** is an argument that goes in a circle—the conclusion and premise say essentially the same thing. Finally, **two wrongs make a right** claims that it is OK to do something to someone else because someone else might do something to you.

Skill Building Until Next Time

- Each of the logical fallacies discussed in this lesson are very common. Listen for them throughout the day. If you listen to talk radio, chances are you'll hear a lot of good examples.
- Think about something that you want someone to do for you. Come up with reasons based on the logical fallacies you learned in this lesson for that person to say yes. Then think of several good, logical reasons. Those are the reasons you should use when trying to convince someone of something.

ANSWERS

1. **NI.** Of course there are other majors that can lead to a good career.

2. **NI.** There are a lot of other ways to put the money to good use.

3. **L.** If there are only two partners, there really are only these three options for getting the work done.

4. **NI.** There are definitely other choices. Raising taxes isn't necessarily the only way to fix the budget deficit. Similarly, not raising taxes doesn't necessarily mean drowning in deficit. There are other ways to address the deficit problem.

5. **NI.** There are many people who are in between. Some people, for example, oppose abortion except in special circumstances, like rape.

6. **SS.** Legalizing marijuana does *not* mean that the legalization of other drugs—especially ones that are much more powerful—will follow.

7. **SS.** Again, X doesn't necessarily lead to Y. There's no reason to believe that three strikes will be reduced to two and then one.

8. **L.** This is a good, logical reason not to drop the class.

9. **C.** This argument doubles back on itself—"you should give me half of that commission" and "I deserve 50%" say the same thing without giving Johnson a reason why he should share half of his commission.

10. **C.** Again, the premise repeats the conclusion. That his "language is confusing" doesn't say any more than what's already been said in the conclusion.

11. **L.** "Good experience" is a good, logical reason for taking the internship.

12. **L.** Preventing people from getting hurt is a good supporting premise for the conclusion here.

13. **C.** Unlike number 12, the premise and the conclusion here say essentially the same thing.

14. Arguments **a** and **c** use the two wrongs make a right fallacy. Argument **b** may look like it does, but look again. In this case, the arguer is saying that people who have *already* murdered should be murdered in turn. This is truly an eye for an eye, not an eye for a maybe.

L·E·S·S·O·N

LOGICAL FALLACIES: DISTRACTERS AND DISTORTERS

13

LESSON SUMMARY

In this final lesson about logical fallacies in deductive reasoning, you'll learn about fallacies that try to divert your attention from the main issue or to distort the issue so you're more likely to accept the argument. These fallacies include *ad hominem*, the red herring, and the straw man.

You are new to your job and are just getting to know your colleagues. One day you are talking with your colleague Ty about how to advance quickly within the company. Later that day, another colleague, Lynette, who'd overheard your conversation, pulls you aside and says, "I heard what Ty was telling you earlier. If I were you, I wouldn't listen to him. He's had the same position for almost 20 years. What does he know about advancing at this company!"

Should you listen to Lynette and ignore Ty's advice?

Since you are new on the job and still just getting to know everyone, you're in a bit of a dilemma here. Who do you trust? Who is more credible? You can't settle those questions yet since you're so new, but what is important to note here is that Lynette has committed a logical fallacy. In this last lesson about logical fallacies in deductive reasoning, you'll learn about **distracters** and **distorters**—fallacies that aim to confuse the issues so that you more easily accept the conclusion of the argument. *Ad hominem* will be discussed first, followed by red herrings and the straw man.

AD HOMINEM

What has Lynette done wrong? After all, if Ty hasn't been promoted in two decades, how *can* he give you good advice about how to move ahead in the company? What Lynette says makes a lot of sense, doesn't it?

Lynette's argument may seem to be logical, but it is not. That's because Lynette is not attacking Ty's *advice;* instead, she's simply attacking *Ty.* This kind of false reasoning is called **ad hominem**, which in Latin means *to the man. Ad hominem* fallacies attack the *person* making the claim rather than the *claim* itself.

An *ad hominem* fallacy can take a variety of forms. You can attack a person, as Lynette does, for his or her personality or actions. You can also attack a person for his or her beliefs or affiliations. For example, you might say, "Don't listen to him. He's a liberal." Or you can attack a person for his or her nationality, ethnicity, appearance, occupation, or any other categorization. For example, imagine someone says to you:

"Of course he's wrong. Someone who dresses like that for work obviously doesn't have a clue about anything."

This is a clear-cut case of *ad hominem.*

Ad hominem aims to distract you from looking at the validity of the claim by destroying the credibility of the person making the claim. But the trouble with *ad hominem* is that it doesn't really deal with the issue of credibility. Just because Ty has held the same position for 20 years doesn't mean he can't give good advice about advancing within the company. In fact, because he's been around for two decades, he's probably seen a lot of people move up the company ladder, so he probably has a very good sense of what those folks did to get ahead.

Furthermore, maybe Ty does have what it takes to move ahead, but for whatever reason has decided to keep his current position. Whatever the case may be, Lynette needs to attack Ty's *argument* about how to advance in the company rather than attacking Ty.

Here's another example:

I've heard Kyra's claim that eliminating grades will improve student performance. But don't buy it. Remember, she's one of those "new age" philosophers.

Here, the speaker attempts to discredit what Kyra says because of who she is, not because of the validity of her claim. It's clear that the speaker doesn't agree with Kyra's philosophies, but that doesn't mean that Kyra's claim about eliminating grades doesn't have merit, and it certainly doesn't mean her argument should automatically be rejected.

Ad hominem fallacies can also work in reverse. That is, the argument can urge you to *accept* someone's argument based on who or what the person is rather than on the validity of the premises. For example, you might read about several different theories of why the dinosaurs became extinct. They all make sense, but you decide the asteroid theory is probably right. Why? Well, all things being equal, the woman arguing for the asteroid theory is from Minnesota, your home state. Of course, her being from Minnesota has nothing to do with the validity of her argument, but because you have something in common with her, that gives her theory a little edge in your eyes. It's not logical, of course, but people commit this kind of *ad hominem* error all the time.

PRACTICE

Read the arguments below carefully. Do they use the *ad hominem* fallacy?

1. Well, if that's what Professor Harvey said, then it must be true.

2. Well, he's got twenty years of experience dealing with consumer complaints, so I think we should trust his advice.

3. I don't think Toni should get the achievement award. Isn't she a member of that feminist group?

4. Manager A to Manager B: "I know we need to address the problems. But Caryn doesn't belong on the review committee. She's just a secretary."

RED HERRING

Just what is a **red herring?** Strange name for a logical fallacy, isn't it? But the name makes sense. Cured red herrings are able to throw dogs off the track of an animal they are chasing. And that's exactly what a *red herring* does in an argument: It takes you off of the track of the argument by bringing in an unrelated topic to divert your attention from the real issue. Here's an example:

Capital punishment is morally wrong, and that's exactly what's wrong with this country. A country can't claim to be a democracy when it can't even keep its people out of jail.

First, break down the argument. What's the conclusion?

Conclusion: Capital punishment is morally wrong.

Now, what are the premises?

Premises:
1. That's what's wrong with this country.
2. A country can't claim to be a democracy when it can't even keep its people out of jail.

Do the premises have anything to do with the conclusion? In fact, do these premises have anything to do with each other? No. Instead of supporting the conclusion, the premises aim to sidetrack you by bringing up at least three different issues:

1. What's wrong with the country.
2. What makes a democracy.
3. Why the country can't keep people out of jail.

Red herrings like these can be so distracting that you forget to look for support for the conclusion the arguer presents. Instead of wondering why capital punishment is morally wrong, you may be wondering what *does* make a country a democracy or why we can't keep people out of jail—that is, if you accept the claim that the country can't keep people out of jail.

Red herrings are a favorite of politicians and people who want to turn potential negative attention away from them and onto others. Watch how it works:

Senator Wolf: "No, I don't believe homosexuals should be allowed in the military. After all, Senator Fox supports it, and he's just trying to get the liberal vote."

Notice how Senator Wolf avoids having to explain or defend his position by shifting the attention away from his claim and onto Senator Fox. Instead of supporting his claim, he leaves the listener wondering if Senator Fox is just out to get more votes. Once again, the red herring tactic throws the argument off track.

PRACTICE

Read the following arguments carefully. Do you see any red herrings? If so, underline them.

5. No, I do not believe that murderers have the right to live. Why should they? The criminal justice system in this country has gotten completely out of control. Criminals of all sorts are getting off scot-free. This has to change!

6. Capital punishment is wrong. We have a law that says it is wrong to kill. We can't have a double standard. If we insist that our citizens should not kill, then our government should not kill, either.

7. I'll tell you why our jails are overcrowded. It's because people like Congressman Jones don't want to raise taxes in their districts.

8. We should eliminate paper money and coins and make all monetary transactions electronic. Everyone would benefit from the convenience of electronic money. And you can see how successful consolidation was in Europe with the Euro.

STRAW MAN

Ever get in a fight with a scarecrow? It's pretty easy to win, when you're fighting a man made of straw. After all, he's not a real man—he falls apart easily and he can't fight back. You're safe and your opponent is a goner. It probably doesn't surprise you that there's a logical fallacy that uses this principle: it sets up the opponent as a straw man, making it easy to knock him down.

Specifically, the **straw man** fallacy takes the opponent's position and distorts it. The position can be oversimplified, exaggerated, or otherwise misrepresented. For example, if someone were arguing *against* tax reform, he might distort the reformers' position by saying:

"The people who support tax reform are only out to get a break in their own capital gains taxes."

Even if getting a tax break is one of the reasons people support tax reform, it can't be the only one—after all, tax reform is a pretty complicated issue. Furthermore, the arguer, using the straw man tactic, presents the reformers as selfish and greedy—in it only for themselves—which makes it easier for the listeners not to want to support their position.

Similarly, if someone were arguing *for* tax reform, she might set up a straw man like the following:

"The folks who oppose tax reform simply don't want to go to the trouble of restructuring the IRS."

True, restructuring the IRS may be one concern of the opponents, but is it their main concern? Is that the real reason they don't support it? Chances are their opposition stems from a number of issues, of which reforming the IRS is only one. Once again, the arguer has misrepresented and oversimplified, making the opponent easy to knock down. In both cases, the reasons for support or opposition are difficult to approve of. One argument claims that the supporters are selfish and the other claims that the opponents are protecting the bureaucracy of the IRS—and neither of these is an admirable position.

Straw men are very commonly used in arguments because people often don't take the time to consider all sides of an issue or because they don't have the courage or counter-arguments to address the complete issue. For example, imagine that someone says:

"Those feminists! They're out to turn all women against men."

Of course, this is a grossly misrepresented "definition" of feminism; indeed, it's difficult to sum up what feminists—or any group, for that matter—believe in just one sentence. But if you present feminists this way, it becomes very easy to avoid coming up with effective counter-arguments; it becomes hard to say that feminism is a good thing.

The trouble is, how do you know if you're being presented with a straw man? What if you've never studied feminism or don't know much about the women's movement? What if you haven't paid much attention to the news about tax reform? In short, how do you know when an opponent is being misrepresented?

Your best bet is to be as informed and educated as possible. And you can do that by reading and listening as much as possible. Watch the news, read the paper, listen to the radio, read magazines—pay attention to things like politics and social issues. The more informed you are, the better you'll be able to see if and when someone is trying to "pull the wool over your eyes" with a straw man.

PRACTICE

Do any of the following arguments use a straw man?

9. Darwinians don't believe in God; Creationists don't believe in science.

10. The Democrats seem to think that it's okay to cut foreign aid and let millions of people in third world countries starve.

11. LeeAnne feels that it's unwise for managers to have their own lounge because it reduces interaction with other employees and limits opportunities for spontaneous learning.

IN SHORT

Now you're armed with three more fallacies to watch out for: *ad hominem,* the **red herring,** and the **straw man.** In *ad hominem,* the arguer attacks the *person* instead of the claim. A red herring brings in an irrelevant issue to throw the argument off track. The straw man presents a distorted picture of the opponent so that the opponent will be easy to knock down. Be on the lookout for these and the other fallacies you've learned as you check for the validity of arguments.

Skill Building Until Next Time

- One way to help you recognize these fallacies is to be sure you can commit them yourself. So, like you did in the previous two lessons, think of several good, logical reasons to support an argument. Then, come up with examples of each of the logical fallacies you learned in this lesson.
- Listen to a call-in talk show on the radio or watch a debate on television, preferably one where audience members are allowed to participate. Listen carefully for the logical fallacies that you've learned. Chances are you'll catch a lot of people trying to get away with false logic.

ANSWERS

1. **Yes.** Unless "it" is about Professor Harvey's grading policies or some other topic on which she is the best authority, accepting her word just because she's a professor is an *ad hominem* mistake.

2. **No.** His experience makes him credible, and that's a good reason to trust his advice.

3. **Yes.** There's no relationship between the achievement award and Toni's affiliations.

4. **Yes.** Just because she's a secretary and not a manager doesn't mean she doesn't have a good perspective on the problem. In fact, because she's "in the trenches," Caryn's ideas are probably very valuable to the managers.

5. No, I do not believe that murderers have the right to live. Why should they? <u>The criminal justice system in this country has gotten completely out of control. Criminals of all sorts are getting off scot-free. This has to change!</u>

6. Capital punishment is wrong. We have a law that says it is wrong to kill. We can't have a double standard. If we insist that our citizens should not kill, then our government should not kill, either. (This argument is logical.)

7. I'll tell you why our jails are overcrowded. <u>It's because people like Congressman Jones don't want to raise taxes in their districts.</u>

8. We should eliminate paper money and coins and make all monetary transactions electronic. Everyone would benefit from the convenience of electronic money. <u>And you can see how successful consolidation was in Europe with the Euro.</u> (The consolidation of different currencies across Europe has nothing to do with eliminating all currencies and making money electronic; these are two distinct issues.)

9. **Yes.** Darwinians and Creationists are misrepresented here. Many Darwinians *do* believe in God and many Creationists are outstanding scientists.

10. **Yes.** The argument misrepresents the Democratic position on foreign aid.

11. **No.** This argument makes good sense—LeeAnne's position is specific and clear.

L · E · S · S · O · N
INDUCTIVE REASONING
14

LESSON SUMMARY

In this lesson, you'll review the difference between deductive and inductive reasoning. You'll also sharpen your inductive reasoning skills by learning how to draw logical conclusions from evidence.

esson 6, "Working with Arguments," talked about the difference between inductive and deductive reasoning. In deductive reasoning, as you know, an argument moves from a conclusion to the evidence (premises) that supports that conclusion. **Inductive arguments,** on the other hand, move from *evidence* to a *conclusion* drawn from that evidence.

As a critical thinker, when you come across a deductive argument, you should examine the validity of the *evidence* for the conclusion. In general, if the evidence is valid, the conclusion—and therefore the whole argument—is a good one. However, in inductive reasoning, the goal is not to test the validity of the evidence. Rather, it is to examine the validity of the *conclusion*. If the conclusion stems logically from the evidence, then the argument can be considered a good one.

But how do you know if the conclusion is logical? In inductive reasoning, the main criterion is to determine the **likelihood** that the premises lead to the conclusion. That likelihood can be judged based on:

1. Good common sense
2. Past experience

Of course, formal logic, involving mathematical symbols, can also help you determine likelihood, but that won't be discussed in this book.

To see how this works, look at this brief inductive argument:

> No matter how many times I repeat the procedure, I keep ending up with results that go against what I'd predicted. I guess our current understanding of this chemical reaction is wrong.

If the premise—that I repeatedly end up with results that contradict my hypothesis—is true, is it reasonable to conclude that my understanding of the chemical reaction needs rethinking? Well, are consistent but unexpected results likely to cause scientists to rethink theories? Based on common sense and past experience, you can say with confidence *yes*. Is it very likely? Again, you can confidently say *yes*. Therefore, the above is a good inductive argument—a logical conclusion drawn from substantial evidence.

THE SCIENCE OF INDUCTIVE REASONING

Any time someone draws conclusions from evidence, inductive reasoning is being used. Scientists use it all the time. For example, let's say a scientist takes two equally healthy plants of the same size, age, and type. She puts Plant A in a room with a radio that plays only classical music. She puts Plant B in a room with a radio that plays only rock and roll. Both plants receive equal light and water. After six weeks, Plant A has grown six inches. Plant B, on the other hand, has grown only three inches, which is the average (normal) growth rate for these types of plants. She repeats this experiment and gets the same results. Using her inductive reasoning skills, what is the most logical thing for the scientist to conclude?

a. In both cases, Plant B must not have been as healthy to start as Plant A.
b. Plants grow better when exposed to classical music than rock and roll.
c. Rock and roll music stunts plant growth.

Well, common sense would suggest that choice **a** isn't an option, because it is stated that both plants were equally healthy at the start of the experiment. Furthermore, since it is known that Plant B grew at the *normal* rate, then **c** can't be a logical conclusion either. But even without this process of elimination, common sense and the results of the two experiments would point to the conclusion that **b,** plants grow better to classical music than to rock and roll. (This is true, by the way!)

Of course, this conclusion would be even more valid if the scientist repeated the experiment several more times and continued to get the same results. The more she performs the experiment and gets the same results, the stronger her argument will be.

ELEMENTARY, MY DEAR WATSON

Detectives, like scientists, also employ inductive reasoning. In the following excerpt from the story "The Reigate Puzzle," for example, the famous fictional character Sherlock Holmes uses inductive reasoning to solve a tricky crime. By examining a piece of a torn document, he is able to conclude that *two* different men wrote the document, and he's able to determine which of the two men is the "ringleader." Watch how he does it:

"And now I made a very careful examination of the corner of paper which the Inspector had submitted to us. It was at once clear to me that it formed part of a very remarkable document. Here it is. Do you not now observe something very suggestive about it?" [said Holmes.]

"It has a very irregular look," said the Colonel.

"My dear sir," cried Holmes, "there cannot be the least doubt in the world that it has been written by two persons doing alternate words. When I draw your attention to the strong *t*'s of 'at' and 'to,' and ask you to compare them with the weak ones of 'quarter' and 'twelve,' you will instantly recognize the fact. A very brief analysis of these four words would enable you to say with the utmost confidence that the 'learn' and the 'maybe' are written in the stronger hand, and the 'what' in the weaker."

"By Jove, it's as clear as day!" cried the Colonel. "Why on earth should two men write a letter in such a fashion?"

"Obviously the business was a bad one, and one of the men who distrusted the other was determined that, whatever was done, each should have an equal hand in it. Now, of the two men, it is clear that the one who wrote the 'at' and 'to' was the ringleader."

"How do you get at that?"

"We might deduce it from the mere character of the one hand as compared with the other. But we have more assured reasons than that for supposing it. If you examine this scrap with attention you will come to the conclusion that the man with the stronger

hand wrote all of his words first, leaving blanks for the other to fill up. These blanks were not always sufficient, and you can see that the second man had to squeeze to fit his 'quarter' in between the 'at' and the 'to,' showing that the latter were already written. The man who wrote all his words first is undoubtedly the man who planned the affair."

Notice how Holmes looks carefully at the document and uses what he sees to make logical inferences (draw logical conclusions) about the two men responsible for the crime. The difference in the *t*'s indicates two different writers and the uneven spacing of the words indicates who wrote first, thus leading Holmes to conclude that the man who wrote first was the man "who planned the affair."

PRACTICE

Now it is your turn to play detective and use your reasoning skills to draw logical inferences. Look carefully at the information you are provided (the premises) and consider what would be the most logical conclusion to draw from that evidence. You'll find the answers at the end of this lesson.

1. Scott always wears his polka-dot tie when he has a job interview—he says it brings him good luck. He's wearing his polka-dot tie today. You can therefore logically conclude
   a. Scott feels that he needs good luck today
   b. Scott has an interview today
   c. Scott wants to look sharp today

2. Every April, you seem to catch a cold that lasts about three weeks. Your symptoms are always worse when you're outside, even if it's warm. You might conclude

a. you should take extra vitamins in the spring

b. you should dress extra warm, even if it's not cold

c. you have a seasonal allergy

3. Mary, Shelly, and Pam have been friends for years and always do things together. When Mary took some graduate courses, so did Shelly and Pam. When Shelly applied for a promotion, so did Mary and Pam. Pam just decided to quit her job and become a consultant. Therefore

a. Mary and Shelly talked Pam into quitting her job.

b. Mary and Shelly talked Pam into being the first one this time.

c. Mary and Shelly will become consultants also.

d. Mary and Shelly will go into business with Pam.

4. If there was only *one* example of Mary, Shelly, and Pam doing the same thing, would you draw the same conclusion? Why or why not?

5. You walk into your office and notice that your desk drawer, which you always close carefully before you leave at the end of the day, is slightly ajar. Which of the following is the most logical conclusion?

a. The drawer is jammed and unable to close properly.

b. Someone was looking through your desk.

c. Maybe you forgot to close the drawer last night.

d. The drawer is broken and needs to be fixed.

IN SHORT

Inductive reasoning is the process of drawing conclusions from evidence. A good inductive argument is one in which it is very likely that the premises lead to the conclusion. Past experience and good common sense can be used to measure that likelihood.

Skill Building Until Next Time

• Notice how often you use inductive reasoning throughout your day. At home, work, or school, as you travel from place to place, what conclusions do you draw from what you see around you?

• Read a detective story or or murder mystery by authors like Agatha Christie, Sue Grafton, Sir Arthur Conan Doyle, Sara Paretsky, and others. As you read, pay special attention to how detectives use evidence to draw conclusions and figure out "whodunnit."

ANSWERS

1. It would be logical to conclude that **b,** Scott has an interview today because Scott "always" wears his polka-dot tie for interviews. It would also be logical (and maybe a little safer) to conclude that **a,** Scott feels that he needs good luck, whether for an interview, a big meeting, or even a date.

2. The most logical conclusion is **c,** that you have a seasonal allergy. If it happens every year at approximately the same time, your "cold" is clearly related to the change in the environment. Furthermore, April, experience tells you, is a time when many plants start to bloom, releasing pollen into the air. It might not hurt to take extra vitamins, but you're most likely suffering from rose fever.

3. Based on the fact that it's already happened twice in similar circumstances, you could logically conclude that **c,** Mary and Shelly will become consultants also. There isn't any evidence of all three being together when one of them does a given thing or of two pressuring the third, so **a** and **b** are not the most logical conclusions. Choice **d** is a possibility, but there isn't any evidence that all three are in the same type of business, or that they'd like to work together, so this isn't the safest bet.

4. If we had only one example of Mary, Shelly and Pam doing the same thing, it would *not* be logical to come to the same conclusion. Though it's only a difference of one instance, if it happened twice, and both times a different woman "started" the trend among her friends, it is logical to conclude that the pattern would complete itself with Pam becoming a consultant and the others following suit—though we don't have enough instances to state that it's *very* likely. But with only one example, we don't have enough evidence to conclude that this would be likely at all.

5. Unless your drawer is terribly overstuffed, and if you clearly recall closing your drawer the night before, **b** is the most logical conclusion. If the drawer were broken, **d,** you would have known.

JUMPING TO CONCLUSIONS

15

LESSON SUMMARY

Just as there are logical fallacies to beware of in deductive reasoning, there are several logical fallacies to look out for in inductive reasoning. This lesson will show you how to recognize and avoid those fallacies.

Your roommate, Sheila, tells you she has good news: "Sarah, Vaughn, and Vladimir haven't even graduated yet, and they've each already gotten several job offers. The job market sure is terrific these days!"

Oops. Sheila has just been caught jumping to conclusions.

Inductive reasoning, as you know, is all about drawing conclusions from evidence. But sometimes people draw conclusions that aren't quite logical. That is, they draw conclusions too quickly or base them on the wrong kind of evidence. This lesson will introduce you to three such logical fallacies in inductive reasoning: *hasty generalizations, biased generalizations,* and *non sequiturs.*

HASTY GENERALIZATIONS

A **hasty generalization** is a conclusion based on too little evidence. That is, in a hasty generalization, you come to a conclusion about X, but you've come to that conclusion too quickly: you haven't seen enough examples or instances of X for a strong argument. In other words, the sample of the population you're examining (X, or the target population) is too small. Remember, the strength of an inductive argument lies in the likelihood that the conclusion will be true. If you've only seen a few instances of X, then the likelihood that the conclusion you reached based on those few instances is true of the whole population is not very strong.

Sheila's conclusion about the job market is a perfect example. Sheila draws a conclusion about the job market based only on the experience of three job seekers. Given her target population (all job seekers in the country), her sample size is far too small. As a result, the likelihood that her conclusion is true—that the job market *is* terrific—is not very strong. However, if Sheila were to get a hold of statistics about job placement rates for current graduates in colleges all around the country, and all of those statistics showed that graduates were getting job offers, then her conclusion would no longer be hasty. Her sample size is much larger and the likelihood that her conclusion is valid is therefore much stronger.

Here's another example of a hasty generalization. This one should be a little more obvious:

Raed goes to job interviews at two very large companies and a very small one. He finds the environment at both large firms stuffy and uninspiring. He finds the atmosphere at the small company friendly and encouraging. He tells his roommate, "I'm only going to interview at small firms from now on. Large companies just don't have the right environment for me."

Raed has really done himself a disservice with this hasty generalization. True, there are differences between work-

ing for large and small firms, but the environment differs from company to company for many different reasons; size is only one factor. Large companies can have relaxed, creative atmospheres, and there can be great variation in atmosphere from department to department. Similarly, small companies can be quite stuffy and restrictive. Raed has made generalizations about small and large firms based on a very small sample.

Hasty generalizations have a lot in common with stereotypes. In the case of stereotypes, conclusions about an entire group are drawn based upon a small segment of that group. Likewise, hasty generalizations draw conclusions about something based on too small a sample—three job seekers, two or three interviews.

PRACTICE

Are any of the following hasty generalizations? You'll find the answers at the end of this lesson.

1. Student A to Student B, second week of the semester: "All the poems we've read so far in Poems of the Renaissance are about love and religion. I guess that's what most poets wrote about in those days."

2. Student A to Student B, final week of the semester: "All the poems we read in Poems of the Renaissance are about love and religion. I guess that's what most poets wrote about in those days."

3. Both Jessie and Teresa went to all-girl high schools and they're at the top of their class. All-girl high schools must be better than co-ed high schools.

BIASED GENERALIZATIONS

In a recent opinion poll, a whopping 85% of people surveyed said they oppose gun control. If most Americans feel this way (85%!), you think, maybe you should think twice about your position on the issue. Shouldn't you?

Unfortunately, what you haven't been told is that the only people who were surveyed were members of the National Rifle Association.

The problem with such a survey (and there will be more on surveys in Lesson 18, "Numbers Never Lie") is that the pool of people it surveyed was *biased*. After all, the NRA is an organization that fights to maintain the right to bear arms. Therefore the conclusion, that most Americans oppose gun control, is biased as well; it's based on a survey of biased respondents and cannot be representative of Americans as a whole.

Biased generalizations can be made without surveys, of course. Whereas a hasty generalization is a conclusion drawn from a sample that is too small, a biased generalization is any conclusion based on a sample that is biased—that is, a sample that is not representative of the target population. As a result, the conclusion you draw isn't likely to hold true for the target population. For example, your roommate's conclusion about the job market is not only a hasty generalization, it's also a biased one. Her sample is three new college graduates; not all job seekers are college graduates, for one thing, and many have advanced degrees and/or years of experience in their fields. If Sarah, Vaughn, and Vladimir are all computer science majors, then the generalization is even more biased, because the three students represent an even smaller segment of the overall target population (all types of jobs available). Thus, any valid conclusion about the job market—which includes blue, white, and "other" collar workers—cannot be based on the experience of three graduating college seniors.

> **Hasty Generalization:** Sample size is too small
> **Biased Generalization:** Sample size is not representative of target population

For example, imagine you tell a friend that you're taking a class next fall with Professor Jenkins.

"Professor Jenkins?!" your friend replies. "She's terrible. I got an F in her class."

Should your friend's reaction change your mind about taking the class? Probably not. Your reasoning skills should tell you that your friend's conclusion about Jenkins might be biased. If he got an F in her class, he isn't likely to have a very good an opinion of her.

Let's look at another example. Read the following inductive argument carefully:

All of my friends say fraternities are a waste of time. So I guess you shouldn't bother trying to join one if you don't want to waste your time.

How could this be a biased generalization? Write your answer below.

If this conclusion is based on evidence from biased sources, then the generalization (the conclusion) is biased. For example, if those friends who say that fraternities are a waste of time are also friends who had wanted to be in a fraternity but had not been invited to join, then they're likely to have a negative (biased) opinion of fraternities. And they're therefore not representative of the target population—not all fraternity members are going to feel this way. Hence, this conclusion would be biased.

On the other hand, how could this be a *reliable* inductive argument? Write your answer below.

If all the friends were members of a fraternity, then this would be a much more reliable conclusion. If all the friends were members of different fraternities rather than the same one, it'd be even more reliable; their conclusion would represent a broader range of experience.

To avoid being biased, then, conclusions should be drawn only from a sample that's truly representative of the subject at hand. An inductive argument about student involvement on campus, for example, should be based on evidence from *all types* of students, not just those on the Student Affairs Committee.

PRACTICE

Are any of the following biased generalizations? You'll find answers at the end of this lesson.

4. I've been following the editorials and letters to the editor in *The Freeport Gazette*. It looks like no one in Freeport is in support of the freeway proposal.

5. All of John Donne's poems are about love or religion. I guess that's all Renaissance poets wrote about.

6. Student struggling in a class: "I asked everyone in the class. They all say the professor is too hard to understand. We're all going to have to work hard to do well."

NON SEQUITUR

A third inductive reasoning fallacy is the *non sequitur*. A ***non sequitur*** is a conclusion that does not follow logically from its premises. The problem with this fallacy is that too much of a jump is made between the premises and the conclusion. Here's an example:

Johnson is a good family man. Therefore, he will be a good politician.

It's great that Johnson is a good family man, but his devotion to his family does not necessarily mean that he'll be a good politician. Notice that this argument *assumes* that the qualities that make "a good family man" also make a good politician—and that's not necessarily, or even probably, the case. Many good family men are lousy politicians, and many good politicians are not particularly devoted to their families. The argument makes a leap—a big one—that defies logic. It's certainly possible that Johnson will be a good politician, but solely judging from the premises, it's not *likely*.

Here's another example of a *non sequitur*:

The prospect was very happy with our presentation. We should get the account.

This *non sequitur* assumes that prospects happy with the presentation will become clients. This may sometimes be true, but it is certainly not always the case. This is a *non sequitur* combined with some wishful thinking. As it stands, it's not a very strong argument. However, you can correct the *non sequitur* by filling in the gaps in the logic of the argument as follows:

The prospect was very happy with our presentation. **Most prospects who are happy with the presentation become clients.** We should get the account.

If you add the missing premise above, then the fallacy is removed and you have a much more valid argument. However, if that premise is not true, then you can see that you have a weak argument.

Similarly, you could correct the first example of a *non sequitur* by adding the following premise:

Johnson is a good family man. **Most good family men make good politicians.** Therefore, he will be a good politician.

By adding this premise, you come to see that the argument isn't very strong since the premise you added to make the original *non sequitur* a logical argument is a premise that is not likely to be true. And if that premise isn't true, the conclusion cannot be true, either.

Some *non sequiturs* follow the pattern of reversing the premise and conclusion. Look at the following argument, for example:

People who succeed always have clear goals. Sandra has clear goals, so she'll succeed.

Here's the argument broken down:

Premise 1: People who succeed always have clear goals.
Premise 2: Sandra has clear goals.
Conclusion: Sandra will succeed.

Though at first glance the example may seem reasonable, in actuality, it doesn't make logical sense. That's because Premise 2 and the conclusion *reverse* the claim set forth in Premise 1. When parts of a claim are reversed, the argument does not stay the same. It's like saying that geniuses often have trouble in school, so someone who is having trouble in school is going to be a genius, and that's just not logical.

In Sandra's case, your critical thinking and reasoning skills should also tell you that simply because she set clear goals for herself doesn't mean they'll be achieved; hard work and dedication are also factors in the formula for success. Furthermore, the definition of *success* is something everyone determines for him- or herself.

PRACTICE

Are there any *non sequiturs* in the arguments below? You'll find answers at the end of this lesson.

7. Paula got straight A's in her science classes. She'll make a great doctor.

8. That car is a stick shift. Most stick shift cars get better gas mileage than automatics. You'll probably get better gas mileage if you get a stick.

9. Rasheed is a good accountant and he didn't even like math in school. You don't like math, so you'd make a good accountant, too.

10. What assumptions do the two *non sequiturs* above make?

IN SHORT

When it comes to inductive arguments, you need to be on the lookout for three kinds of logical fallacies. **Hasty generalizations** draw conclusions from too little evidence—a sample that is too small. **Biased generalizations,** on the other hand, draw conclusions from *biased* evidence—a sample that is not representative of the target population. Finally, **non sequiturs** jump to conclusions that defy logic; they make assumptions that don't hold water.

ANSWERS

1. Hasty generalization. This may turn out to be true, but two weeks into the semester is too soon to tell. Also, Student A should remember that the professor is selecting from a large body of work and may be excluding poems about other topics.

2. Since Student A has now completed a course in Poems of the Renaissance, she has seen a much larger sample of poetry from the time period. Especially because Student A has used the word most, this is a valid inductive generalization.

3. Hasty generalization. This conclusion is based on a very small sample.

4. Yes, this is a biased generalization. Even if most folks in Freeport read the *Gazette*, that doesn't mean that the people who write the editorials and letters to the editor are representative of the entire population of Freeport. And if there are several different papers in Freeport, this generalization is even less reliable.

5. While John Donne is one of the most famous Renaissance poets, he's not representative of all the poets of the time. This is another biased generalization.

6. Though this student is struggling, if she's asked everyone in the class and they're all having trouble understanding the professor too, her conclusion is probably fair.

7. Yes, this is a *non sequitur*.

8. No *non sequiturs* here.

9. *Non sequitur.*

10. Argument number 7 assumes that people who are good students in science are also good doctors. But being a good doctor requires more than getting good grades. It also involves years of training, an ability to handle crises, skill in dealing with patients, and much more.

    In argument number 9, the second premise and conclusion reverse the first premise. Just because you don't like math doesn't mean you'll make a good accountant; what happened to Rasheed won't necessarily happen to you.

L·E·S·S·O·N

16

USING INDUCTIVE REASONING TO DETERMINE CAUSES

LESSON SUMMARY

This lesson will discuss the inductive reasoning approach to determining causes. It will also go over some of the common mistakes people make when determining cause and effect.

An old story has it: The final exam in a philosophy class asked students just one question: "Why?" A student responded simply, "Why not?"

Why things happen, why things are the way they are, how things came to be—these questions are often answered by a specific type of inductive argument, the **causal argument.**

In a causal argument, you look at the evidence ("My colleagues have been very distant with me lately") and draw a conclusion based on that evidence ("Maybe they're upset that I got a promotion"). Then, as in any inductive argument, you test the validity of the conclusion.

Casual arguments and explanations, like any argument, need to be evaluated, and there are several strategies for evaluating causes. Similarly, just as arguments can use false reasoning, there are also logical fallacies that can be committed in causal arguments. This chapter will start with the two main strategies for determining cause and the fallacies that often go with them.

DETERMINING CAUSE

When you are presented with an effect and want to inductively determine the cause, there are generally two techniques you can use: to look for what is different, and to look for what is the same.

LOOKING FOR THE DIFFERENCE

Your car wasn't running well on Wednesday. Normally you use Ultra-Plus gasoline from the station down the street, but on Tuesday, you were low on gas and on cash, so you pulled into a station near your office and got half a tank of the cheapest brand. On Thursday, you went back to your regular station and filled up with your normal gas. By Friday, the car was running fine again. You did nothing else to your car, and nothing else was out of the ordinary.

So what caused the problem?

If you guessed the cheap gasoline, you're probably right. Though there are many things that can go wrong with a car and only a thorough inspection could tell for sure, the given evidence points to the cheap gas as the culprit. Why? Because the cheap gas is the **key difference**. Let's recap the facts: Your car ran well on your usual gas. When you changed the brand and grade, your car didn't run well. When you went back to your usual gas, your car ran fine again. The difference? The gasoline. Therefore, it's logical to conclude that the gasoline caused your car to run less smoothly.

Though in this example it's obvious that the gasoline was the key difference, it isn't always so easy to determine causes. Look at the following argument for example:

Every day for the past three months, you've been getting coffee from Lou's Deli, right around the corner from your office. One day, however, Lou's is closed,

so you decide to try Moe's Deli across the street. You get your coffee and go to work. An hour later, you have a terrible stomach ache. The next day, Lou's is open again and you get your usual coffee. You feel fine the rest of the day. "It must've been Moe's coffee that gave me that stomach ache yesterday," you conclude.

This does seem like a logical conclusion, based on the evidence. After all, what's different between today and yesterday? It was Moe's coffee that was the difference, so it was Moe's coffee that caused your stomach ache. Right?

Not necessarily. It is quite possible that Moe's coffee did indeed cause your stomach ache. However, this conclusion can't be accepted without reservation—you can't say it's *likely* that Moe's coffee is to blame—until you ask a key question:

Were there any other relevant differences that may have caused the stomach ache?

In other words, you need to consider whether there could have been something else that caused your stomachache. For example, maybe late the night before you ate extra spicy Chinese food. Or maybe you were really nervous about a big meeting that day. Or maybe you skipped breakfast and had an upset stomach to begin with. Any one of these phenomenons could have caused the stomach ache.

The more possibe causes there are, the less confident you should be that Moe's coffee is the culprit. However, if there isn't anything else unusual that you can think of, and especially if you get sick if you try Moe's again, then it's much more likely that Moe's is to blame. Either way, before you pinpoint your cause, be sure to consider whether or not there could be other relevant differences.

PRACTICE

Answer the following questions carefully. Answers are given at the end of this lesson.

1. Is the following a logical causal argument? Why or why not?

Since the state raised taxes on liquor three years ago, teenage drinking has dropped considerably. Clearly, higher prices for alcohol will reduce teenage drinking.

2. You're taking an exam in your calculus class. You understand the material, but you've been doing poorly on your exams. Recently, however, you learned several deep-breathing techniques, which you employ during the exam. You also recently started a new habit: reviewing your notes every week instead of just before exams. When you get your exam back, you see that you scored 98 out of 100. You conclude:
   a. your new study habit has paid off
   b. the test was easy

   c. your deep breathing enabled you to relax and do better on the test
   d. both **a** and **c**

LOOKING FOR THE COMMON DENOMINATOR

Sometimes the cause can be determined not by looking for what's different, but by looking for what's the *same*—that is, something that each incident has in common. Take the following scenario, for example:

Jason has been having trouble sleeping a few nights a week. On the nights when he can't sleep, he notices that the neighbor's dog is always barking and howling. Jason concludes that his trouble sleeping is due to the dog.

Jason has used a logical approach to determine the cause of his insomnia. He's looking for a pattern—something that is consistent with the nights he can't sleep. Because he hears the dog barking and howling on all of those nights, it could be that the dog is pre-

---

The Difference Between Correlation and Causation

Sometimes what seems to be a **causal** relationship is actually a **correlative** relationship. **Causation** claims that X *brought about* Y; Y would not exist or exist in its current form without the occurrence of X. **Correlation,** on the other hand, claims that two phenomena vary in relation to each other. That is, if X correlates to Y, Y might increase every time there's an increase in X. Or Y might *decrease* every time there's an increase in X. The point is that when X changes, there's a corresponding change in Y. For example, if teenage smoking also went down when the price of alcohol went up, you might argue that there is a correlation between the rate of smoking among teenagers and the rate of drinking. What this does *not* claim, however, is that the increase in the price of alcohol *caused* the decrease in smoking. Similarly, because so many factors are involved, you can't even safely say the price increase *caused* the drop in the rate of teenage drinking. You can, however, duly note the correlation and examine the phenomena further.

- **Causation:** X causes Y to happen.
- **Correlation:** When X changes, there is a corresponding change in Y, but this does not mean that X caused Y. Both changes are probably caused by a combination of other factors.

venting him from getting his beauty sleep. The dog is the **common denominator** for all of these occasions.

Just as it is important to be careful not to overlook other possible differences, however, it's important to remember to look for other possible common denominators. Before Jason concludes that his sleeplessness is caused by the barking dog, he should carefully consider whether there might be anything else in common on those nights that he can't sleep.

So let's complicate the situation just a bit by adding more evidence from which to draw your conclusion:

Jason has been having trouble sleeping a few nights a week. On the nights when he can't sleep, he notices that the neighbor's dog is always barking. He also realizes that the rough nights are always nights that he hasn't had a good day at work. Those are also nights that he skipped his normal exercise routine. What's causing Jason to have trouble sleeping?

a. the dog barking
b. not having a good day at work
c. not exercising
d. none of the above

Can you answer this question with confidence? Probably not. That's because each of these answers is a legitimate possibility. Each item occurs on each of the nights Jason can't sleep. Just like the coffee wasn't the only thing different in the previous scenario, here the dog isn't the only common denominator. There are many possibilities. If you're to confidently say which of these is the cause, you need to pinpoint just one event in common with all the bad nights or to determine which of these factors might be having the greatest effect on Jason. For example, if Jason knew that the dog

barked *every* night—even on those nights when he is able to sleep—then the barking could be eliminated as an option. Similarly, if Jason also skips his exercise on nights when he *can* sleep, then choice **c** could be eliminated. But until more evidence is given, and the other possibilities can be eliminated, none of the choices can be chosen over the others.

PRACTICE

Are the following causal arguments logical? Why or why not? You'll find answers at the end of this lesson.

3. In our last five fundraisers, Mackenzie Wilson has been the emcee, and we've raised record amounts each year. The Board wants us to try someone new, but Mackenzie is the key to our fundraising success.

4. Professor Climes notices that a number of her students seem to perform very well on lab reports but do poorly on exams. She surveys her students and finds that all of those who do well on lab reports but poorly on exams are majoring in the fine arts. As fine arts majors, the students report, they rarely take exams; their grades are based on projects (paintings, compositions, etc.) and papers. Professor Climes concludes that their lack of practice in taking exams is causing them to do poorly on her tests.

POST HOC, ERGO PROPTER HOC

Nina, who'd always dressed rather plainly, decided it was time to jazz up her wardrobe. She went shopping and bought a closet full of new, brightly colored clothing.

Two weeks later, she was promoted at work. "I know how important it is to look good," she told her friend, "but I had no idea that what I wore to work could make such a difference. Just changing my wardrobe finally got me that promotion I'd been waiting for!"

Nina deserves congratulations, of course, but not for her reasoning. What's wrong with her logic here?

Nina has committed the ***post hoc, ergo propter hoc*** inductive reasoning fallacy. *Post hoc, ergo propter hoc* literally means *after this, therefore because of this.* Nina has assumed that because her promotion came *after* she changed her wardrobe, her promotion was *caused* by her change in wardrobe. Maybe, just maybe, her appearance did have something to do with it. But in all likelihood, there were several other causes for her promotion. She'd probably been doing good work for years, for one thing, and the position to which she had been promoted may not have been vacant before. There may be several other good reasons as well.

Of course, cause and effect *is* a chronological structure—the cause must come before the effect—but remember that you need to consider other possible causes. Just because A comes before B doesn't mean there's a logical connection between the two events.

Here's another example of *post hoc*:

After the Citizens First bill was passed, crime in this area skyrocketed. Funny how the bill that was supposed to *reduce* crime actually *increased* it!

Notice how this argument assumes that because the Citizens First bill came first and the rise in crime came second, one *caused* the other. But proving that there's a causal link between the two events would not be easy, especially since an increased crime rate could be caused by many different factors. In fact, a figure as complicated as crime rate is probably caused by a mul-

titude of factors. What else can you think of that might have caused the increase in crime?

Other possible causes:

You may have listed other possible causes like the following:

- An increase in unemployment
- A recession
- A change in population in the area
- A reduction in the police force

In fact, because human society is so complex, most social issues have multiple causes. In all likelihood, the increase in crime was caused by a combination of these, and possibly other, factors, some of which may have a clear correlative relationship, but arguing cause is much more complicated. That is, you could more confidently say when unemployment increases and the police force decreases, crime usually increases. This does not, however, claim that a rise in unemployment and a decrease in the police force *cause* an increase in crime. There are probably several other forces at work. The Citizens First bill, unless it specifically cut jobs and reduced the police force, is not to blame. It may have come first, but it's not necessarily the cause.

PRACTICE

Do any of the following causal arguments commit the *post hoc* fallacy?

5. I used to drink four or five cups of coffee a day and I had lots of headaches. Now that I quit drinking coffee, my headaches are gone.

6. A Democrat takes office and next thing you know, unemployment is on the rise. If you want to keep unemployment rates down, vote for a Republican governor next time.

7. Before meeting with his manager for his first annual review, Bradley ran into an old colleague, Jones, toward whom he felt a great deal of animosity. Bradley was let go shortly afterwards. "It was seeing Jones that ruined it for me," he said. "I was really upset and had a lousy meeting with my manager."

THE CHICKEN OR THE EGG?

"I'll tell you where all the violence in society is coming from," your neighbor says to you one day. "It's caused by all the violence on television."

Maybe—but not necessarily. Before you agree, consider that your neighbor could just as easily have argued:

"All that violence on television is just a reflection of all the violence you see in society."

Which argument is correct? Does television violence cause violence in society, or is violence in society the reason there is so much violence on television?

Clearly, both arguments try to simplify a topic that's very complicated. What also makes this case problematic is that it's hard to tell what came first, violence on television or violence in society. It's the old **chicken or egg dilemma**—Y could have caused X as much as X could have caused Y. You need to think carefully about the relationship between the two events before you come to any conclusions.

Here's another example:

Lucy feels more confident because she aced her last two exams.

True, getting good grades can boost your self-esteem. But it is also true that someone who feels confident is likely to perform better on an exam than someone who does not. So this is another case where cause and effect could go either way: Lucy's increased confidence could be caused by her good grades, but it's equally likely that her good grades were caused by her increased confidence. In such a case, it's best to suspend judgment about the cause until more information is known.

PRACTICE
Read the following carefully. Are any guilty of taking sides in the chicken or egg dilemma?

8. People don't have family values anymore. That's because so many people get divorced these days.

9. Since Linda started exercising, she feels a lot better about herself.

10. There are so many computer manufacturers because the cost of computer technology is so low.

IN SHORT

There are two main approaches to determining causes in inductive reasoning: looking for what's different and looking for the common denominator. It is important to remember to look for other possible differences or common causes. Causal arguments should avoid the **post hoc, ergo propter hoc** fallacy, which assumes that because A came before B, A *caused* B. Finally, some causal arguments fall into the **chicken and egg** trap, where the argument that A caused B is just as strong as the argument that B caused A. Think carefully before accepting such an argument.

Skill Building Until Next Time

- Be on the lookout this week for errors in causal reasoning. People are often quick to assign cause and neglect to think about other possible differences or common denominators. See if you can catch others—or even yourself—making these mistakes and correct them.
- Read some history. Historical texts explore cause and effect in detail, and they'll help you see just how complicated causes can sometimes be. This will help you realize how careful you need to be when evaluating cause and effect.

ANSWERS

1. No, this is not a logical causal argument. Because there are probably many other relevant factors, the best you can say is that there is a correlation between taxes on liquor and the rate of teenage drinking. (See page 121 for a definition of correlation.)

2. The best answer is **c.** Since you'd generally performed poorly on exams but understood the material, the most likely conclusion is that you were a poor test taker, and that your deep-breathing techniques enabled you to relax and do well on the exam. It's also possible that your new study habit paid off, but since you understood the material before, this isn't as powerful a difference as your new relaxation technique.

3. A good emcee can make or break a fundraising campaign. If Mackenzie has been the emcee for the last five years and each year has been a great success, by all means, bring Mackenzie back again this year. But be careful not to attribute the success entirely to Mackenzie, because there are several other possible causes. Perhaps the organization's programs and events have been very successful; perhaps the organization has been managed better in the last five years; perhaps one or two donors have been particularly generous in the last few years. There can be many reasons for the success of the fundraising campaign.

4. While Professor Climes has found a common thread among the students who are doing poorly on her exams, she may not be making a logical argument here. While these students may be "out of practice" with their test-taking strategies, there are several other possible causes. Perhaps the students are just weak test takers and would

do poorly even if they took exams regularly; perhaps they just have other priorities and neglect to study for the exams. These are just two possible reasons for this phenomenon.

5. This seems like a reasonable argument, not a *post hoc* error. Part of what makes this logical is the general knowledge that caffeine can cause headaches in some drinkers as its effect wears off.

6. *Post hoc.* Because unemployment rose after a Democrat took office does not mean that the Democrat *caused* the rise in unemployment. In fact, many factors contribute to a change in the rate of unemployment, and it may take several years for some of those factors to have an effect on unemployment. The governor's policies and programs certainly affect unemployment, but so do economic trends, business decisions, and many other factors. Still, if you're going to blame the politician, it's probably safer to blame the governor in office *before* the incumbent Democrat.

7. *Post hoc.* True, Bradley may not have had a good interview, but it's safe to assume that Bradley's manager based his or her review on Bradley's performance throughout the year, not just on the interview.

8. Guilty. It's just as easy to argue that "So many people get divorced these days because people don't have family values anymore." As with any social issue, there are certain to be multiple causes.

9. Though it *is* possible to argue the reverse, it's pretty likely that Linda's exercise is indeed responsible for her increased self-esteem.

10. Guilty. This is another chicken and egg dilemma. The low cost of technology could just as likely be the result of so many different companies working to develop more cost-effective products and procedures. This case needs further investigation.

WHY DID IT HAPPEN?

LESSON SUMMARY

In this lesson, you'll learn how explanations are different from arguments. You'll also learn the criteria for determining whether the explanation you're being offered is good or not.

You are an hour and a half late to work. The moment you walk through the door, your boss calls you into his office. "Where have you been?" he asks. "I demand an explanation."

Explanations are very closely related to arguments, but they're not quite the same thing. Whereas an argument generally aims to convince you that a certain claim is true, an explanation aims to convince you *why* a claim is true. For example, compare the following passages:

1. You should get to registration as early as possible. Students who are late usually don't get the classes they want.
2. He didn't get the classes that he wanted because he didn't get to registration early enough.

The first example is an argument. The writer is trying to convince you to get to registration early (conclusion) because students who are late usually don't get the classes they want. The second example, on the other hand, is an explanation. The writer here is telling you *why* someone didn't get the classes that he wanted—because he didn't get to registration early enough.

So explanations are different from arguments. But what does this have to do with critical thinking and reasoning skills?

Well, just as you will be presented with arguments of all types every day of your life, you will also be presented with explanations of all kinds on a daily basis. And just as you need to evaluate arguments carefully before you decide whether or not to accept them, you should also evaluate explanations carefully before you decide whether or not they're valid.

When it comes to explanations, there are four criteria that you should look for:

1. Relevance
2. Testability
3. Circularity
4. Compatibility with existing knowledge

RELEVANCE

One of the first tests any explanation should undergo is the test for **relevance.** Is the explanation that is provided clearly relevant to the thing being explained? That is, is there a clear and obvious connection between the thing and the explanation?

For example, you might say to your boss, "I'm late because the electricity went off during the night and my alarm never went off." Is that relevant? Absolutely. Your ability to arrive on time depends upon your ability to wake up on time. However, an explanation like the following is *not* relevant:

"I'm late because the price of gas went up again this week."

Though you may need to buy gas to get to work, the fact that the price of gas went up has no bearing on your ability to get to work on time. This should be obvious, but that doesn't prevent people from offering irrelevant explanations.

PRACTICE

1. Provide another relevant and another irrelevant reason for being late to work. You'll find answers at the end of this lesson.

Relevant:

Irrelevant:

Read the following explanations carefully. Are they relevant (R) or irrelevant (I)?

_____ **2.** I failed the class because it's at 8:00 on Monday mornings.

_____ **3.** I failed the class because I missed the final exam.

_____ **4.** I failed the class because there's never any parking near campus.

TESTABILITY

You may not be a scientist, but you've certainly performed some experiments in your life. You may have bought different brands of soap, for example, to see which brand was better for your skin type. Or you may have tried different cold medicines to see which worked best for you. This type of experimenting enables you to explain why you make some of the choices that you do: "I use SharpImage toner cartridges for my printer because they give me the cleanest, sharpest printouts." This explanation is one that can be tested. It therefore passes the next test of validity for explanations: **testability**.

Testability is as important as relevance when it comes to evaluating explanations. If someone provides an explanation that is impossible to test, then you should be highly suspicious. An **untestable explanation** is one that is impossible to verify through experimentation. And that's precisely why you should be on guard.

For example, imagine that someone offers you the following explanation:

Global warming is caused by invisible, weightless particles attracted by the Earth's gravity.

Is there any way to test this explanation? If the particles can't be seen or weighed, and if the universe they come from is invisible, then no one can prove that this is or *isn't* the cause. It can't be verified and it can't be refuted. The theory is untestable.

Here's another example:

We met because we were meant to meet.

Is there any way to test this explanation? No. There's no test for fate, after all. Though it may be romantic, this is an untestable—and therefore invalid—explanation.

PRACTICE

Read the following explanations carefully. Are they testable (T) or untestable (U)? You'll find answers at the end of this lesson.

_____ **5.** You got the promotion because we were all pulling for you.

_____ **6.** There is fossil evidence of evolution because God wants to test our faith.

_____ **7.** The restaurant is doing better because it changed the menu.

_____ **8.** Our dreams are our subconscious desires.

CIRCULARITY

Back in Lesson 12, "Logical Fallacies: The Impostors," you learned about circular reasoning: arguments that double back on themselves because the conclusion and the premise say essentially the same thing. Explanations can be circular, too. You might say to your boss, for example:

I'm late because I didn't get here on time.

That's a **circular explanation**. "I'm late" and "I didn't get here on time" say essentially the same thing. The "explanation" simply restates the situation rather than explaining it, and that doesn't make for a valid explanation.

Here's another example:

The inflation was caused by an increase in prices.

Notice that "inflation" and "increase in prices" are essentially the same thing. Once again, this is an explanation that goes in a circle. The explanation does not offer any insight as to how or why the situation occurred.

PRACTICE

Read the explanations below carefully. Identify explanations that pass (P) the test for logic and those that fail (F) because they are circular.

_____ **9.** He has insomnia because he has trouble sleeping.

_____ **10.** She's a genius because she's gifted.

_____ **11.** They work well together because they share the same goals.

_____ **12.** Brendan doesn't do will in math because he's not good with figures.

_____ **13.** We're way over budget for this project because we've spent too much on development.

More Practice

Write two circular explanations of your own on another piece of paper. To see if they're really circular, use this test: is the explanation (usually the part that comes after the word *because*) really the same as the thing you're supposed to be explaining?

COMPATIBILITY WITH EXISTING KNOWLEDGE

Your boss didn't like your "I'm late because I didn't get here on time" explanation, so you try again:

"I'm late because my teleportation machine broke down."

Chances are that even if your boss is a "Star Trek" fan, he won't find your explanation very amusing—and he definitely won't find it valid. Why? Because he knows there's no such thing as a teleportation machine—at least not yet. You get to work by car, bus, train, or some other currently available means of transportation, but not by teleportation. Your explanation goes against what he knows to be true, so he has every right to be very suspicious of your explanation.

Scientific discoveries and technological break-throughs often surprise people and sometimes shatter theories that were long thought to be true. Remember, people once believed that the earth was flat. Still, in everyday life, it's a good idea to be wary of explanations that go against what you know from your past experience and from your education. For example, if you know that the office copier was just fixed this morning, and your assistant says she didn't finish the copies you requested because the copier is broken, you have good reason to doubt the validity of her explanation. Similarly, if your neighbor tells you that gravity is actually caused by a giant U-shaped magnet located at the center of the earth, you should be highly suspicious since his explanation conflicts with accepted scientific theories about the makeup of the earth's interior.

Some explanations, however, may sound odd or surprising to you without necessarily contradicting what you know from your experience and education. In this case, it's probably best to suspend your judgment anyway, until you can verify the explanation. Like *tentative truths*, these explanations might be valid, but you need to learn more before accepting them as true.

For example, imagine you are the boss and an employee tells you, "I'm late because there was a major accident on the freeway." Now you know that things like this happen. Depending upon the credibility of that employee, you could:

- Accept that explanation as fact
- Accept that explanation as a tentative truth
- Reject the explanation, especially if that employee has a history of lying

In a case like this, the credibility of the person offering the explanation is a key factor. But it's important to note that this is not an untestable explanation. You could listen to traffic reports on the radio, talk to other employees who take that freeway, or watch for a report of an accident in tonight's paper to find out if the employee was telling the truth.

PRACTICE

Consider the following explanations and their sources. Are they acceptable? Why or why not?

14. Your long-time co-worker and friend: "I'm sorry I can't stay late to help you with the Myerson report tomorrow. I have a doctor's appointment and I can't reschedule again."

15. Your local garage mechanic: "Your car broke down because your transmission is shot. It's going to need a lot of work."

16. Neighbor: "I drink a bottle of wine a day because it's good for your health."

IN SHORT

Explanations, much like arguments, need to meet certain criteria before you should feel comfortable accepting them. To be valid, an explanation should be **relevant**—clearly related to the event or thing in question—and **testable**—able to be verified in some way. **Circular explanations**—ones that double back on themselves like circular arguments—should be rejected, and you should be careful about accepting explanations that contradict your knowledge or accepted theories.

Skill Building Until Next Time

- Pay attention to the explanations around you: at home, at work, at school, and on TV. See how often you find people offering explanations that don't meet the criteria discussed in this lesson.
- Comedies—in both literature and film—often get laughs from the explanations characters offer when they find themselves in undesirable situations. The next time you read a comic story or novel or watch a comic film, be on the look out for bad explanations. Are they amusing because they're irrelevant? Circular? Untestable? Just plain absurd?

ANSWERS

1. Answers will vary. You might have written something like the following:

   Relevant: My car broke down and I had to wait an hour for the tow truck.
   Irrelevant: I need a new car radio.

   One important thing to keep in mind about explanations is that an explanation can pass the relevancy test and still not be a *good* explanation. For example, "I'm late because last night I was at a SuperBowl party" is not a *good* explanation, but it is a *relevant* explanation—because you were out late, you didn't get up in time for work.

2. **R.** Maybe this isn't such a good reason, but the fact that it's an early class could have an effect on someone's grades, unless he or she is a morning person, in which case this would be irrelevant.

3. **R.** Missing a final exam definitely has a bearing on passing a class.

4. **I.** The parking situation—no matter how the student gets to class—should have no bearing on how he or she does in the class itself.

5. **U.** There's no way to test whether their "pulling for" you had any affect on your getting a promotion. However, if they had all *recommended* you, that would be a valid explanation.

6. **U.** There's no way to test the validity of this explanation.

7. **T.** Patrons could be surveyed to see why they go to the restaurant.

8. **U.** As of yet, we are unable to determine what really goes on in our subconscious mind.

9. **F.** "Insomnia" and "has trouble sleeping" are two ways of saying the same thing.

10. **F.** Once again, being a genius and being gifted are just about the same, so there's really no explanation given here.

11. **P.** This explanation gives a reason that they work well together.

12. **F.** That Brendan "doesn't do well in math" and that "he isn't good with figures" says the same thing.

13. **P.** This explanation shows why the project is over budget.

14. If you've worked with this person a long time and consider her a friend, then this explanation should be acceptable.

15. The acceptability of this explanation would depend partly upon how much you know about cars. A ruined transmission is a very costly repair. If you don't know much about cars and don't know your mechanic very well, it might do you good to get a second opinion.

16. Unacceptable. Studies have shown that a glass of wine a day may have some health benefits, but your knowledge and experience should tell you that a bottle of wine a day is excessive and can lead to serious health consequences.

"NUMBERS NEVER LIE"

LESSON SUMMARY

Statistics are often used to strengthen arguments—but they aren't always trustworthy. This lesson will show you how to judge the validity of statistics and how to make sure that numbers you provide are credible.

here's strength in numbers. Whether on the battlefield or the boardroom, the more people you have fighting for a cause, the more likely you are to win. There's strength in numbers in arguments, too—statistics generally carry more weight, sound more valid, than opinions. That's because numbers look concrete, factual, and objective. But numbers are not always to be trusted. Like words, numbers can be—and often are—manipulated. As a critical thinker, you need to beware of the kinds of tricks people can play with numbers, and you need to know how to evaluate surveys, statistics, and other figures before you accept them as valid.

FIRST THINGS FIRST: CHECK THE SOURCE

One of your first priorities when you come across a figure or statistic is to consider the source. Where is this information coming from? You need to know the source so you can consider its credibility.

Figures are often cited without any indication of their source. When you come across such a statistic, you should automatically sound an alarm. When there's no source acknowledged, that figure could come from anywhere. Here's an example:

Eighty percent of all Americans believe that there is too much violence on television.

Our immediate reaction might be to say "Eighty percent! That's an impressive statistic." But because this claim does not indicate a source, you have to fight your instinct to accept the statistic as true. The question "Who conducted this survey?" must be answered in order for you to be able to assess the validity of the figure. A figure that isn't backed by a credible source isn't worth much and can't be accepted with confidence. Unfortunately, since not everyone out there is honest, you have to consider that the claimant could have made it up to give the *appearance* of statistical support for his argument.

If the claimant does provide a source, then the next step is to consider the credibility of that source. Remember, to determine credibility, look for evidence of bias and level of expertise.

Here's that statistic again attributed to two different sources:

1. According to Parents Against Television Violence, 80 percent of Americans believe that there is too much violence on TV.
2. According to a recent University of Minnesota survey, 80 percent of Americans believe there is too much violence on TV.

Would you accept the statistic as offered by source number 1? How about by source number 2?

While both sources may have a respectable level of expertise, it should be acknowledged that the people who conducted the university study probably have a higher level of expertise. More importantly, the source in number 1—Parents Against Television Violence—should cause some concern. Is a group such as PATV likely to be biased in the issue of television violence? Absolutely. Is it possible, then, that such an organization could offer false or misleading statistics to support its cause, or that it might conduct a highly biased survey? Yes. Would it be wise, therefore, to accept this statistic only with some serious reservations? Yes.

The university's study, however, is much more likely to have been conducted professionally and accurately. Scholarly research is subject to rigorous scrutiny by the academic community, so the university's findings are probably quite accurate and acceptable. There's less reason to suspect bias or sloppy statistical methods.

PRACTICE

Evaluate the following statistics. Are the sources credible? Why or why not? You'll find answers at the end of this lesson.

1. A survey conducted by the California Produce Association shows that four out of five people disapprove of the Farm Redistribution Act.

2. According to the Federal Drug Administration, 67 percent of Americans worry about toxic chemicals on their fruits and vegetables.

THE IMPORTANCE OF SAMPLE SIZE

In the ideal survey or opinion poll, *everyone* in the population in question would be surveyed. But since this is often impossible, researchers have to make do by interviewing a **sample** of the population. Unfortunately, this means that their results do not always reflect the sentiment of the entire population.

Obviously, the larger the sample size, the more reflective the survey will be of the entire population. For example, say you want to find out how Catholics across the country feel about legalizing marriage between homosexuals. If there are six million Catholics in America, how many should you survey? Six? Six hundred? Six thousand? Sixty thousand? Six hundred thousand?

Of course, how many people you survey depends upon the time and money you have to invest in the survey. But under no circumstances would six or sixty be sufficient—these numbers are simply far too small a percentage of the population you're surveying. However, 60,000 is much better; though it only touches one percent of the Catholic population, it's quite a substantive number. Six hundred thousand, on the other hand, reaches 10 percent of that population, making it much more likely that the results of your survey accurately reflect the sentiments of the population as a whole.

On NBC TV's news magazine "Dateline," commentator Stone Phillips often ends the show with the results of a "Dateline" opinion poll. Before announcing the results, however, "Dateline" tells its viewers exactly how many people were surveyed. That is, "Dateline" lets you know the exact sample size. This practice helps make the results "Dateline" produces more credible and enables you to judge for yourself whether a sample is large enough to be representative of the sentiments of the entire country.

You're probably wondering how much is enough when it comes to sample size. There's no hard and fast rule here except one: the larger your sample size, the better. The bigger the sample, the more likely it is that your survey results will accurately reflect the opinions of the population in question.

PRACTICE

3. Read the following situation carefully and answer the question that follows. You'll find answers at the end of this lesson.

You're conducting a survey of students to determine how many support the administration's proposal for a dry campus. There are 5,000 students. You've set up a small polling booth in the student union. After how many responses would you feel you have a sample large enough to reflect the opinion of the entire student body?

a. 50
b. 100
c. 500
d. 1,000

REPRESENTATIVE VS. BIASED SAMPLES

Let's say you want to conduct that survey but don't have any budget. Since you belong to a fraternity with 100 members, you decide to simply poll the members of your fraternity. Will your results accurately reflect the sentiment on your campus?

Regardless of how often your fraternity hosts parties and how its members feel about drinking, it'd be nearly impossible for your survey results to accurately reflect the sentiments of the student body. Why? Because your sample is not **representative** of the population whose opinion you wish to reflect. In order for your sample to be representative, it should include *all* the various groups and subgroups within the student population. That is, the people in your sample group should represent the people in the whole group. That means, for one thing, that you need to survey members from several different fraternities, not just yours. In addition, your sample group needs to include members from *all* different campus organizations—student government, sororities, political groups, athletics, various clubs, and so on.

Furthermore, to be truly representative, the sample should include respondents from these groups in approximately the same **proportion** that you would find them on campus. That is, if 50 percent of the students belong to fraternities or sororities, then approximately 50 percent of your respondents should be members of fraternities or sororities. If 20 percent are members of an athletic group, then approximately 20 percent of your respondents should be athletes, and so on. In this way, your survey results are more likely to be proportionate to the results you'd get if you were able to survey everyone on campus.

But how do you get a representative, proportionate sample for larger populations such as six million Catholics or one billion Chinese? Because the range of respondents is so wide, your best bet is to get a **random** sample. By randomly selecting participants, you have the best chance of getting a representative sample because each person in the population has the same chance of being surveyed.

As a result you'll get responses from the various sub-groups in the population in approximately the same proportion in which they exist in the population. Samples that are representative, proportionate, and random help prevent you from having a **biased** sample. Imagine you read the following:

In a survey of 6,000 city residents, 79 percent of the respondents say that the Republican mayor has done an outstanding job.

This claim tells us the sample size—6,000—which is a substantive number. But it doesn't tell how the 6,000 residents were chosen to answer the survey. Because the

political affiliation and socioeconomic standing of the respondents could greatly influence the results of the survey, it is important to know if those 6,000 people are varied enough to accurately reflect the sentiment of an entire city.

For example, if all of those 6,000 surveyed were Republicans, of course the percentage of favorable votes would be high; but that doesn't tell much about how people from other political parties feel. Survey another 6,000 residents—say, Democrats and people on welfare—and you'd come up with a much, much lower number. Why? Because members of this sample group, because of their socio-economic status and/or their political beliefs, might be biased *against* a Republican mayor. Thus, it's critical that the sample be as representative as possible, including both Democrats and Republicans, the wealthy of the city and the poor, in approximately the same proportion in which they exist in the population.

How do you know, though, that a survey has used a representative sample? Surveys that have been conducted legitimately will generally be careful to provide you with information about the sample size and population so that their results are more credible. You might see something like the following, for example:

- In a recent survey, 500 random shoppers were asked whether they felt the Food Court in the mall provided sufficient selection.
- A random survey of 3,000 men between the ages of 18 and 21 found that 72 percent think either the drinking age should be lowered to 18 or the draft age should be raised to 21.

Notice how these claims let you know exactly who was surveyed.

Special Note

Beware of call-in surveys and polls that are conducted by mail or that otherwise depend upon the *respondents* to take action. Results of these surveys tend to be misleading because those who take the time to return mail-in surveys or make the effort to call, fax, or E-mail a response are often people who feel very strongly about the issue. To assume that the opinions of those people who feel strongly about the issue represents how the entire population feels is dangerous because it's not very likely that *most* people in the population feel that way.

PRACTICE

Evaluate the following claims. Do the surveys seem to have representative samples, or could the samples be biased?

4. Topic: Should campus security be tighter?
Population: Female students
Sample: Women who have been victims of crimes on campus

5. Topic: Is there sufficient parking in the city?
Population: City residents and visitors
Sample: People randomly stopped on the street in various districts within the city

6. Topic: Should Braxton Elementary extend school hours until 4:00 P.M.?
Population: All parents of children in Braxton Elementary
Sample: Members of the PTA

COMPARING APPLES AND ORANGES

In 1972, a Hershey's chocolate bar cost only 5 cents. Today, the same bar costs at least 50 cents. That's an increase of over 1,000 percent!

This figure sounds awful, doesn't it? But is it really as horrendous as the math makes it seem? Not quite.

The problem with this claim is that while the actual price of a Hershey's bar may have increased 1,000%, it's not a fair comparison. That's because 5 cents in 1972 had more market value than 5 cents today. In this situation, the actual costs can't legitimately be compared. Instead, the costs have to be compared after they've been *adjusted for inflation*. Because there has been such a time span and the value of the dollar has declined in the last 25 years, maybe 50 cents today is actually cheaper than 5 cents was in 1972.

It's important, therefore, to analyze comparisons like this to be sure the statistics are indeed comparable. Any monetary comparison needs to take into consideration market value and inflation. When dealing with figures other than money, however, there are other important concerns. For example, look at the following argument:

In 1988, there were 100 arrests for misdemeanors in Regal County. In 1997, there were 250. That's an increase of 150 percent in just ten years. Crime in this county is getting out of control!

What's wrong with this argument? Clearly, there has been a sharp increase in the number of misdemeanor arrests in the last decade. But what the claim *doesn't* tell is that during the same time period, the population of Regal County increased by 250 percent. Now what does that do to the previous argument?

If the population increased from 100,000 to 350,000, is the increase in arrests still evidence that "Crime in this county is getting out of control"? No. As a matter of fact, this means that the number of arrests per capita (that is, per person) has actually *decreased*. Thus, once again, this is a case of comparing apples to oranges because the population in 1998 is so different from the population in 1988.

You should beware of any comparison across time, but the same problems can arise in contemporary comparisons. Take the following statistics for example:

St. Mary's Hospital has fewer cesarean sections per delivery than St. Ann's.

If you want to have a natural birth, should you go to St. Mary's to deliver your baby? Not necessarily. Consider this: St. Ann's Hospital specializes in difficult births and high-risk pregnancies. Because their pool of patients is different, the number of cesarean sections is also going to be different. Apples and oranges.

PRACTICE

Do the following statistics compare apples and oranges, or are they fair comparisons? You'll find answers at the end of this lesson.

7. I bought this house in 1964 for just $28,000. Now it's worth $130,000. What a profit I've made!

8. Students at Regal County Community College are smarter than those at Braxton County. The average GPA for Regal students is 3.2, while the average for Braxton students is 2.9.

9. The total per capita income in Jewel County, adjusted for inflation, went up 12 percent in the last two years.

IN SHORT

The truth about statistics is that they can be very misleading. When you come across statistics, check the source to see whether or not it's credible. Then look for a sample size and decide whether it's substantial. Look for evidence that the sample is representative or random and not biased. Finally, beware of statistics that compare apples to oranges by putting two unequal items side by side.

Skill Building Until Next Time

- Look for survey results in a trustworthy newspaper with a national circulation, like *The New York Times, Washington Post,* or *San Francisco Chronicle.* Notice how much information they provide about how the survey was conducted. Then, look for survey results in a tabloid or a less credible source. Notice how little information is provided and check for the possibility of bias.
- Think about a survey that you would like to conduct. Who is your target population? How would you ensure a representative sample? How large should your sample be?

ANSWERS

1. This source has a respectable level of expertise, but you should worry about its potential for bias. Given the source, there is a possibility that the survey could have been manipulated to show such a high disapproval rating.

2. Because the FDA is a government organization whose credibility rests on its awareness of food and drug dangers to American citizens, this statistic can probably be trusted.

3. Five hundred (**c**) responses would probably be sufficient to give you a good idea of the overall sentiment on campus. If you could get 1,000 responses, however, your results would be much more accurate. Both 50 and 100 are far too small for sample sizes in this survey.

4. The sample in this survey is clearly biased. If only women who have been victims of crime on campus are surveyed, the results will certainly reflect a dissatisfaction with campus security. Furthermore, unless this is an all-female college, the sample is not representative.

5. The sample in this survey is representative. People randomly stopped on the street in various parts of the city should result in a good mix of residents and visitors with all kinds of backgrounds and parking needs.

6. This sample is not representative. Only a limited number of parents are able to find the time— or have the desire—to join the PTA. Parents who hold down two jobs, for example, aren't likely to be members, but their opinion about the extended school day is very important.

7. Apples and oranges. When this figure is adjusted for inflation, you might see that the house has the same market value.

8. The fairness of this comparison depends upon several factors. Are the courses equally rigorous? Are the grading standards the same? If so, then it's probably a fair comparison (apples to apples). But in all likelihood, there are differences in academic rigor and standards which vary not just from department to department but from teacher to teacher. Thus, this is probably an unfair apples to oranges comparison.

9. Fair.

L·E·S·S·O·N

PUTTING IT ALL TOGETHER

LESSON SUMMARY

This lesson puts together the strategies and skills you've learned throughout this book, particularly in Lessons 11–18. You'll review the key points of these lessons and practice both your inductive and deductive reasoning skills.

efore you begin "putting it all together," let's review what you've learned in the second half of this book. If you'd like a quick review of the first half, turn to Lesson 10.

LESSON 11: LOGICAL FALLACIES: APPEALS TO EMOTION

You learned that people will often try to convince you to accept their claims by appealing to your emotions rather than your sense of reason. They may use *scare tactics*, *flattery*, or *peer pressure*, or they may appeal to your sense of *pity*.

LESSON 12: LOGICAL FALLACIES: THE IMPOSTORS

You learned about four logical fallacies that pretend to be logical but don't hold water. *No in-betweens* claims that there are only two choices when, in fact, there are many. The *slippery slope* fallacy argues that if X happens, then Y will follow, even though X doesn't necessarily lead to Y. *Circular reasoning* is an argument that goes in a circle—the premises simply restate the conclusion. And *two wrongs make a right* argues that it's okay to do something to someone else because someone else might do that something to you.

LESSON 13: LOGICAL FALLACIES: DISTRACTERS AND DISTORTERS

You learned how to recognize three common logical fallacies that divert your attention and distort the issue. An *ad hominem* fallacy attacks the *person* instead of attacking the claims that that person makes. A *red herring* distracts you by bringing in an irrelevant issue while the *straw man* distorts the opponent's position so that the opponent is easier to knock down.

LESSON 14: INDUCTIVE REASONING

You learned that inductive reasoning is the process of drawing logical conclusions from evidence. You also learned that a good inductive argument is one in which it is very *likely* that the premises lead to the conclusion.

LESSON 15: JUMPING TO CONCLUSIONS

You learned to distinguish between good inductive reasoning and inductive fallacies like *hasty generalizations,* which draw conclusions from too little evidence. *Biased generalizations* draw conclusions from biased evidence, and *non sequiturs* draw conclusions that don't logically follow from the premises.

LESSON 16: USING INDUCTIVE REASONING TO DETERMINE CAUSES

You learned the two inductive reasoning approaches to determining cause: looking for what's different and looking for the common denominator. You learned to look for other possible differences and common causes and to watch out for the *post hoc, ergo propter hoc* fallacy—assuming that because A came before B, A *caused* B. You also learned how to avoid the "chicken or egg" causal argument.

LESSON 17: WHY DID IT HAPPEN?

You practiced evaluating explanations for validity. You learned that explanations must be relevant and testable and that you should reject explanations that are circular. You also learned the importance of being wary of explanations that contradict your existing knowledge or accepted theories.

LESSON 18: "NUMBERS NEVER LIE"

You learned that numbers can be very misleading. You practiced checking statistics for a *reliable source,* an adequate *sample size*, and a *representative sample*. You also learned how to recognize statistics that compare "apples and oranges."

> **If any of these terms or strategies sound unfamiliar to you, STOP. Take a few minutes to review whatever lesson is unclear.**

PRACTICE

Now it's time to pull all of these ideas together, add them to what you learned in the first half of the book, and tackle the following practice exercises. You'll find answers at the end of this lesson.

Read the following passage carefully and then answer the questions that follow.

Ban the Cloning of Human Beings! Now is the time to create a permanent ban on the cloning of human beings. If we don't act now, before you know it there will be thousands of companies exploiting the cloning process to make armies of worker-drones and dozens of dictators making their own armies of killers. Would you want to be cloned by a mad scientist? Research shows that over 80 percent of the American people say no!

1. Which deductive reasoning fallacy is used in this passage?
   a. scare tactics
   b. dysphemisms
   c. slippery slope
   d. red herring

2. The phrase "armies of killers" is a
   a. euphemism
   b. dysphemism
   c. false dilemma
   d. loaded question

3. The question "Would you want to be cloned by a mad scientist?" is a
   a. euphemism
   b. dysphemism
   c. false dilemma
   d. loaded question

4. What is wrong with the claim that "Research shows that over 80 percent of the American people say no!"?
   a. It doesn't tell who the researchers are.
   b. It doesn't give the sample size.
   c. The sample may be biased.
   d. both **a** and **b**
   e. **a, b,** and **c**

5. Does this argument offer any facts? If so, write the facts below. If not, are there any claims you can accept as tentative truths, or is each claim an opinion?

What, if anything, is wrong with the following?

6. I know Barry said you should buy a Camry, but what does Barry know? He believes in UFOs.
   a. begging the question
   b. *ad hominem*
   c. *non sequitur*
   d. circular reasoning
   e. nothing wrong

7. The last three times we went to that restaurant the service was slow and the food was lousy. It's gone down the tubes. Let's go somewhere else instead.
   a. biased generalization
   b. hasty generalization
   c. *non sequitur*
   d. two wrongs make a right
   e. nothing wrong

8. Amos wasn't upset that we borrowed his Walkman, so I'm sure he wouldn't mind if we borrowed his car.
   a. biased generalization
   b. *non sequitur*
   c. two wrongs make a right
   d. nothing wrong

9. I never tried meditation until just the other day, and now look—I win the lottery! Meditation sure makes good things happen!
   a. *post hoc, ergo propter hoc*
   b. untestable explanation
   c. the chicken and the egg dilemma
   d. nothing wrong

10. The bridge is in terrible condition because it is falling apart.
    a. untestable explanation
    b. circular explanation
    c. irrelevant explanation
    d. nothing wrong

Read the following passage carefully and then answer the questions that follow.

Anna's apartment has been robbed. Only her valuable jewels, which she kept carefully hidden, have been stolen. Anna claims that the only people who knew where the jewels were hidden were her mother and her fiancée, Louis. Anna recently lost her job. Louis claims he was working at the time of the robbery and that he never told anyone else about the hiding place. Louis's boss and a co-worker vouch for Louis, claiming he was indeed at work at the time of the robbery. However, Louis's boss was not with Louis the entire time—he left before Louis's shift was over. Louis's boss was convicted of insurance fraud several years ago. Anna's insurance on the jewelry is worth several hundred thousand dollars. She recently had the jewels re-appraised.

11. Which of the following is the most logical conclusion to draw from the above evidence?
    a. Anna fabricated the whole thing for the insurance money.
    b. Louis stole the jewels and is paying his boss to cover for him.
    c. Anna, Louis, and Louis's boss are all in it together for the insurance money.
    d. Anna is an innocent victim of a plot by Louis and his boss to steal her jewelry and sell it while Louis helps her spend her insurance money.

12. Is Louis's boss's testimony credible? Why or why not?

How did you do? (You can check your answers at the bottom of the page.) If you got all of the answers correct, congratulations! Good work. If you missed a few, you might want to use the chart below to guide your review.

If you missed:	Then study:
Question 1	Lesson 12
Question 2	Lesson 5
Question 3	Lesson 5
Question 4	Lesson 18
Question 5	Lesson 3
Question 6	Lesson 13
Question 7	Lesson 15
Question 8	Lesson 15
Question 9	Lesson 16
Question 10	Lesson 17
Question 11	Lesson 15
Question 12	Lesson 4

CONGRATULATIONS!

You've completed 19 lessons and have seen your critical thinking and reasoning skills improve. If you want to work on your problem-solving skills, or if you need advice on preparing for and taking exams, read Lesson 20.

To see how much you've improved in your critical thinking skills, take the post-test.

ANSWERS

1. The answer is **c,** slippery slope. Notice how the passage claims that if X happens ("if we don't act now"), then Y will automatically follow. But not banning cloning now doesn't mean that thousands of companies will start "exploiting the cloning process to make armies of worker-drones" and that "dozens of dictators" will be "making their own armies of killers." Of course, this is possible, but it's certainly not necessarily true.

2. "Armies of killers" is a **b,** dysphemism, replacing the neutral word *soldiers* with something far more negative.

3. "Would you want to be cloned by a mad scientist?" is a **d,** loaded question. The word *mad* makes it difficult to answer *yes* to this question, because who knows what a "mad scientist" would do with you (or your clones). Right?

4. The problem with this claim is **e—a, b,** and **c.** The claim isn't supported by information about the researchers, the sample size isn't given, and there's no way to know if the respondents are biased. Who knows; maybe the sample group included only members of an organization against cloning.

5. Since the statistic can't be accepted as fact, no, the passage does not contain any facts. The statistic can only be accepted as a tentative truth. The rest of the claims are all opinions.

6. This is **b,** *ad hominem.* The argument rejects Barry's claim because of who Barry is (someone who believes in UFOs), not because of why Barry thinks you should buy a Camry.

7. There's really nothing wrong (**e**) with this argument. If the argument was simply "The last time we went . . . ," then the arguer would be guilty of

a hasty generalization—the restaurant probably just had a bad night. But if three times in a row both the service and food were bad, then it's probably not a bad decision to go elsewhere.

8. This is **b,** a *non sequitur.* Just because Amos didn't mind us borrowing his Walkman doesn't mean he won't mind us borrowing his car. There's a big difference between a Walkman and an automobile.

9. This is the **a** *post hoc* fallacy. The arguer claims that because he meditated first and won the lottery second that the meditation *caused* him to win the lottery.

10. This is a **b,** circular explanation. The fact that the bridge "is falling apart" doesn't explain why it's "in terrible condition;" it's simply another way of saying the same thing.

11. The most logical conclusion to draw from this evidence is **c,** that all three of them are in it together. Anna had recently lost her job, so she might be in need of money. The fact that she recently had

her jewelry re-appraised should add to your suspicions, as should the fact that only the jewelry was taken. Furthermore, Louis's boss committed insurance fraud in the past, so his credibility should be doubted. It might be inferred that Louis's boss committed the robbery, since he was not with Louis the entire time Louis was at work. Even if Louis's boss didn't actually commit the robbery, chances are good that his boss was somehow involved in planning the theft. It's logical to assume that Louis stayed at work so that he wouldn't be a suspect, and therefore he needed someone else (like his boss) to commit the actual crime.

12. Louis's boss's testimony should be regarded suspiciously. Because this is probably a case of insurance fraud, and because he was guilty of insurance fraud in the past, he's not a trustworthy witness or alibi.

L·E·S·S·O·N

PROBLEM SOLVING AND TEST-TAKING STRATEGIES

20

LESSON SUMMARY

While logic problems and puzzles can be fun, they can also help determine the direction of your career if you ever have to be tested on your logic and reasoning skills. This lesson will show you what types of questions you'll typically find on such an exam and how to tackle those kinds of questions. You'll also learn general test-taking strategies.

Strong critical thinking and reasoning skills will help you make better decisions and solve problems more effectively on a day-to-day basis. But they'll also help you in special situations, like when you are being tested on your logic and reasoning skills. You may be in a critical thinking class, taking a test that will help you qualify for a job, or applying for a promotion—or maybe you just like to solve logic problems and puzzles for fun. Whatever the case, if you find yourself face to face with logic problems, you'll see they generally come in the form of questions that test your:

- Ability to prioritize issues and create a logical plan of action
- Ability to distinguish good evidence from bad
- Ability to draw logical conclusions from evidence

You've been learning a lot about critical thinking and deductive and inductive reasoning, so you should already have the skills to tackle these kinds of questions. This lesson aims to familiarize you with the format of these kinds of test questions and to provide you with strategies for getting quickly to the correct answer.

CREATING A LOGICAL PLAN OF ACTION

Questions that test your ability to prioritize issues and create a logical plan of action often present you with decision-making scenarios. Though the situation may be foreign to you and the questions may seem complicated, you can find the answer by remembering how to break a problem down into its parts and by thinking calmly and logically about the situation so you can effectively prioritize the issues.

SAMPLE QUESTION

Look, for example, at the following question:

Jonathan wants to run for president of the senior class. In what order should he do the following?
  I. Come up with a catchy campaign slogan
  II. Develop a campaign platform
  III. Find out the procedures and requirements for running for class office
  IV. Create posters and post them all around the school

  a. I, II, III, IV
  b. II, I, IV, III
  c. III, II, I, IV
  d. III, I, II, IV

The problem is already broken down into key parts: now you need to place them in a logical order. Logic should tell you that the best answer here is **c.** Without question, the first thing Jonathan needs to do is find out the proper procedures and requirements for running for class office. Maybe in order to run for president Jonathan must have a grade point average of 3.0. If Jonathan doesn't have that average and hasn't bothered to check the requirements before doing I, II, and IV, he's wasting his time and energy. Logic should also tell you that Jonathan has to develop a campaign platform before he should come up with a slogan and posters. After all, shouldn't his slogan and posters reflect what he plans to do as senior class president? Finally, Jonathan should want to have his slogan—a catchy phrase that can easily be remembered—on all of his posters, so the posters are clearly the last of Jonathan's steps.

EVALUATING EVIDENCE

Logic tests often measure deductive as well as inductive reasoning skills. That's why some questions may ask you to evaluate evidence. Remember, strong evidence for a deductive argument is both *credible* and *reasonable.*

SAMPLE QUESTION

You'll need to keep these criteria in mind and use your common sense to work your way through problems like the following:

Nadine has complained to management that the bathroom facilities in her office reflect a bias against women. Which of the following would provide the strongest support for her claim?

a. That all the women in the office agree with Nadine.

b. That the twenty-five women have only two bathroom stalls whereas the thirty-five men have five urinals and three stalls.

c. That there are 30 percent more men in the office than women.

d. That women usually visit the restroom more frequently than men and take longer per visit.

You should have selected **b** as the best answer. Why? Because **b** provides the most *specific* and *relevant* support for the argument. Though there is strength in numbers and it helps to have all the women supporting her argument, Nadine is more likely to sway management with concrete facts, like the number of stalls per user. It's clear from the evidence provided in **b** that the men's facilities are far more adequate than the women's. Choice **c** isn't the best evidence here because it simply states the difference in male and female employees. Without a direct relationship to the question of the restrooms, this statistic is meaningless. Answer **d,** while it could support Nadine's claim, is not as strong as evidence **b,** because it doesn't directly address the number of facilities.

Now it's your turn.

PRACTICE

Read the following scenario carefully and answer the questions that follow. You'll find answers at the end of this lesson.

City Council member Andrew Anderson claims that the city could save millions of dollars each year by turning services like garbage collection over to private companies.

1. Which of the following would provide the strongest support for Anderson's argument?
   a. statistics showing how much the city spends each year on these services
   b. statistics showing how much comparable cities have saved by farming out these services to private companies
   c. proposals from private companies showing how well they could perform these services for the city and at what costs
   d. a direct comparison of how much the city spends per year on these services and how much the city would save by farming the services out to private companies

2. Which of the following is most likely to work AGAINST Anderson's argument?
   a. statements from citizens protesting the switch from public to private services
   b. statistics demonstrating how much more the average citizen would have to pay for privatization of these services
   c. reports from other cities with privatized services about citizen protests that forced the return to public services
   d. reports from other cities about corruption among privatized service providers

DRAWING CONCLUSIONS FROM EVIDENCE

Many questions you face when you're being tested on your reasoning skills will ask you to draw conclusions from evidence. You've completed several lessons now on inductive reasoning, so you should be quite good at these questions, even if their format is different from what you're used to.

As in the other types of questions, you can help ensure a correct response by using the process of elimination. Given the evidence the question provides, you should automatically be able to eliminate some of the answers.

SAMPLE QUESTION

For example, look at the following question:

A jeep has driven off the road and hit a tree. There are skid marks along the road for several yards leading up to a dead fawn. The marks then swerve to the right and off the road, stopping where the jeep is. The impact with the tree is head-on but the damage is not severe. Based on the evidence, which of the following is most likely what happened?

a. The driver was aiming for the fawn and lost control of the jeep.
b. The driver fell asleep at the wheel and was awakened when he hit the fawn.
c. The driver tried to avoid the fawn and lost control of the jeep.
d. The driver was drunk and out of control.

Given the facts—especially the key fact that there are skid marks—you can automatically eliminate choices a and b. If the driver were aiming for the fawn, he probably wouldn't have hit the brakes and created skid marks. Instead, he probably would have accelerated, in which case his impact with the tree would have been harder and resulted in more damage. Similarly, if the driver had fallen asleep at the wheel and only woken up when he hit the fawn, there wouldn't have been skid marks leading up to the fawn.

So now you're down to two possibilities: c and d. Which is more likely to be true? While it is entirely possible that the driver was drunk, all of the evidence points to c as the most likely possibility. The skid marks indicate that the driver was trying to stop to avoid hitting the fawn. Unsuccessful, he hit the animal and swerved off the road into a tree.

Other questions that ask you to draw conclusions from evidence may vary in format, but don't let their appearance throw you. Just remember to look carefully at the evidence that's provided and eliminate the incorrect answers as you go along.

PREPARING FOR A TEST

Many students get nervous or anxious thinking about taking an upcoming test or final exam, so don't feel you're alone if you experience such feelings. Nervousness is natural—and it can even be an advantage if you know how to channel it into positive energy.

The following pages provide suggestions for overcoming test anxiety both in the days and weeks before the test and during the test itself.

TWO TO THREE MONTHS BEFORE THE TEST

The number one best way to combat test anxiety is to **be prepared.** That means two things: Know what to expect on the test and review the material and skills on which you will be tested.

Know What to Expect

What knowledge or skills will the exam test? What are you expected to know? What skills will you be expected to demonstrate? What is the format of the test? Multiple choice? True or false? Essay? Ask your instructor. If the test isn't for class, go to a bookstore or to the library and get a study guide that shows you what a sample test looks like. Or maybe the agency that's testing you for a job gives out a study guide or conducts study sessions. The fewer surprises you have on test day, the better you will perform. The more you know what to expect, the more confident you will be that you can handle the questions.

Review the Material and Skills You'll Be Tested On

The fact that you are reading this book means that you've already taken this step in regard to logic and reasoning questions. Now, are there other steps you can take? Are there other subject areas that you need to review? Can you make more improvement in this or other areas? If you are really nervous, or if it has been a long time since you reviewed these subjects and skills, you may want to buy another study guide, sign up for a class in your neighborhood, or work with a tutor.

The more you know about what to expect on test day and the more comfortable you are with the material and skills to be tested, the less anxious you will be and the better you will do on the test itself.

THE DAYS BEFORE THE TEST
Review, Don't Cram

If you have been preparing and reviewing in the weeks before the exam, there's no need to cram a few days before the exam. Cramming is likely to confuse you and make you nervous. Instead, schedule a relaxed review of all that you have learned.

Physical Activity

Get some exercise in the days preceding the test. You'll send some extra oxygen to your brain and allow your thinking performance to peak on the day you take the test. Moderation is the key here. You don't want to exercise so much

that you feel exhausted, but a little physical activity will invigorate your body and brain. Walking is a terrific, low-impact, energy-building form of exercise.

Balanced Diet

Like your body, your brain needs the proper nutrients to function well. Eat plenty of fruits and vegetables in the days before the test. Foods that are high in lecithin, such as fish and beans, are especially good choices. Lecithin is a protein your brain needs for peak performance. You may even consider a visit to your local pharmacy to buy a bottle of lecithin tablets several weeks before your test.

Rest

Get plenty of sleep the nights before you take the test. Don't overdo it, though, or you'll make yourself as groggy as if you were overtired. Go to bed at a reasonable time, early enough to get the number of hours you need to function **effectively**. You'll feel relaxed and rested if you've gotten plenty of sleep in the days before you take the test.

Trial Run

At some point before you take the test, make a trial run to the testing center to see how long it takes you to get there. Rushing raises your emotional energy and lowers your intellectual capacity, so you want to allow plenty of time on test day to get to the testing center. Arriving ten or fifteen minutes early gives you time to relax and get situated.

Motivation

Plan some sort of celebration—with family or friends, or just by yourself—for after the test. Make sure it's something you'll really look forward to and enjoy. If you have something to look forward to after the test is over, you may find it easier to prepare and keep moving during the test.

TEST DAY

It's finally here, the day of the big test. Set your alarm early enough to allow plenty of time to get to the testing center. Eat a good breakfast. Avoid anything that's really high in sugar, such as donuts. A sugar high turns into a sugar low after an hour or so. Cereal and toast, or anything with complex carbohydrates is a good choice. Eat only moderate amounts. You don't want to take a test feeling stuffed! Your body will channel its energy to your digestive system instead of your brain.

Pack a high-energy snack to take with you. You may have a break sometime during the test when you can grab a quick snack. Bananas are great. They have a moderate amount of sugar and plenty of brain nutrients, such as potassium. Most proctors won't allow you to eat a snack while you're testing, but a peppermint shouldn't pose a problem. Peppermints are like smelling salts for your brain. If you lose your concentration or suffer from a momentary mental block, a peppermint can get you back on track. Don't forget the earlier advice about relaxing and taking a few deep breaths.

Leave early enough so you have plenty of time to get to the test center. Allow a few minutes for unexpected traffic. When you arrive, locate the restroom and use it. Few things interfere with concentration as much as a full bladder. Then find your seat and make sure it's comfortable. If it isn't, tell the proctor and ask to change to something you find more suitable.

Now relax and think positively! Before you know it the test will be over, and you'll walk away knowing you've done as well as you can.

COMBATING TEST ANXIETY

Okay—you know what the test will be on. You've reviewed the subjects and practiced the skills on which you will be tested. So why do you still have that sinking feeling in your stomach? Why are your palms sweaty and your hands shaking?

Even the brightest, most well-prepared test takers sometimes suffer bouts of test anxiety. But don't worry; you can overcome it. Below are some specific strategies to help you.

Take the Test One Question at a Time

Focus all of your attention on the one question you're answering. Block out any thoughts about questions you've already read or concerns about what's coming next. Concentrate your thinking where it will do the most good—on the question you're answering now.

Develop a Positive Attitude

Keep reminding yourself that you're prepared. In fact, since you've read this book, you're probably better prepared than most others who are taking the test. Remember, it's only a test, and you're going to do your **best**. That's all anyone can ask of you. If that nagging drill sergeant voice inside your head starts sending negative messages, combat them with positive ones of your own. Tell yourself:

- "I'm doing just fine."
- "I've prepared for this test."
- "I know exactly what to do."
- "I know I can get the score I'm shooting for."

You get the idea. Remember to drown out negative messages with positive ones of your own.

If You Lose Your Concentration

Don't worry about it! It's normal. During a long test it happens to everyone. When your mind is stressed or overexerted, it takes a break whether you want it to or not. It's easy to get your concentration back if you simply acknowledge the fact that you've lost it and take a quick break. You brain needs very little time (seconds, really) to rest.

Put your pencil down and close your eyes. Take a deep breath, hold it for a moment, and let it out slowly. Listen to the sound of your breathing as you repeat this two more times. The few seconds that this takes is really all the time your brain needs to relax and get ready to focus again. This exercise also helps you control your heart rate, so that you can keep anxiety at bay.

Try this technique several times in the days before the test when you feel stressed. The more you practice, the better it will work for you on the day of the test.

If You Freeze

Don't worry about a question that stumps you even though you're sure you know the answer. Mark it and go on to the next question. You can come back to the "stumper" later. Try to put it out of your mind completely until you come back to it. Just let your subconscious mind chew on the question while your conscious mind focuses on the other items (one at a time—of course). Chances are, the memory block will be gone by the time you return to the question.

If you freeze before you even begin the test, here's what to do:

1. Do some deep breathing to help yourself relax and focus.
2. Remind yourself that you're prepared.
3. Take a little time to look over the test.
4. Read a few of the questions.
5. Decide which ones are the easiest and start there.

Before long, you'll be back on track.

TIME STRATEGIES

One of the most important—and nerve-wracking—elements of a standardized test is time. You'll only be allowed a certain number of minutes for each section, so it is very important that you use your time wisely.

Pace Yourself

The most important time strategy is **pacing yourself**. Before you begin, take just a few seconds to survey the test, making note of the number of questions and of the sections that look easier than the rest. Then, make a rough time schedule based on the amount of time available to you. Mark the halfway point on your test and make a note beside that mark of what the time will be when the testing period is half over.

Keep Moving

Once you begin the test, **keep moving**. If you work slowly in an attempt to make fewer mistakes, your mind will become bored and begin to wander. You'll end up making far more mistakes if you're not concentrating. Worse, if you take too long to answer questions that stump you, you may end up running out of time before you finish.

So don't stop for difficult questions. Skip them and move on. You can come back to them later if you have time. A question that takes you five seconds to answer counts as much as one that takes you several minutes, so pick up the easy points first. Besides, answering the easier questions first helps to build your confidence and gets you in the testing groove. Who knows? As you go through the test, you may even stumble across some relevant information to help you answer those tough questions.

Don't Rush

Keep moving, but **don't rush.** Think of your mind as a seesaw. On one side is your emotional energy. On the other side is your intellectual energy. When your emotional energy is high, your intellectual capacity is low. Remember how difficult it is to reason with someone when you're angry? On the other hand, when your intellectual energy is high, your emotional energy is low. Rushing raises your emotional energy and reduces your intellectual capacity. Remember the last time you were late for class or work? All that rushing around probably caused you to forget important things—like your notes for a meeting. Move quickly to keep your mind from wandering, but don't rush and get yourself flustered.

Check Yourself

Check yourself at the halfway mark. If you're a little ahead, you know you're on track and may even have a little time left to check your work. If you're a little behind, you have several choices. You can pick up the pace a little, but do this *only* if you can do it comfortably. Remember—**don't rush!** You can also skip around in the remaining portion of the test to pick up as many easy points as possible. This strategy has one drawback, however. If you are marking a bubble-style answer sheet, and you put the right answers in the wrong bubbles—they're wrong. So pay close attention to the question numbers if you decide to do this.

AVOIDING ERRORS

When you take the test, you want to make as few errors as possible in the questions you answer. Here are a few tactics to keep in mind.

Control Yourself

Remember that comparison between your mind and a seesaw? Keeping your emotional energy low and your intellectual energy high is the best way to avoid mistakes. If you feel stressed or worried, stop for a few seconds. Acknowledge the feeling (Hmmm! I'm feeling a little pressure here!), take a few deep breaths, and send yourself a few positive messages. This relieves your emotional anxiety and boosts your intellectual capacity.

Directions

In many standardized testing situations a proctor reads the instructions aloud. Make certain you understand what is expected. If you don't, **ask.** Listen carefully for instructions about how to answer the questions and make certain you know how much time you have to complete the task. Write the time on your test if you don't already know how long you have to take the test. If you miss this vital information, **ask for it.** You need it to do well on your test.

Answers

This may seem like a silly warning, but it is important. Place your answers in the right blanks or the corresponding ovals on the answer sheet. Right answers in the wrong place earn no points—they may even lose you points. It's a good idea to check every five to ten questions to make sure you're in the right spot. That way you won't need much time to correct your answer sheet if you have made an error.

Choosing the Right Answers by Process of Elimination

Make sure you understand what the question is asking. If you're not sure of what's being asked, you'll never know whether you've chosen the right answer. So figure out what the question is asking. Be sure to read the questions and answer choices carefully. A simple word like *not* can turn a right answer into a wrong answer. If the answer to the question isn't readily apparent, look for clues in the answer choices. Notice the similarities and differences in the answer choices. Sometimes this helps to put the question in a new perspective and makes it easier to answer. If you're still not sure of the answer, use the process of elimination. First, eliminate any answer choices that are obviously wrong. Then reason your way through the remaining choices. You may be able to use relevant information from other parts of the test. If you can't eliminate any of the answer choices, you might be better off to skip the question and come back to it later. If you can't eliminate any answer choices to improve your odds when you come back later, then make a guess and move on.

If You're Penalized for Wrong Answers

You **must know** whether there's a penalty for wrong answers before you begin the test. If you don't, ask the proctor before the test begins. Whether you make a guess or not depends upon the penalty. Some standardized tests are scored in such a way that every wrong answer reduces your score by one fourth or one half of a point. Whatever the penalty, if you can eliminate enough choices to make the odds of answering the question better than the penalty for getting it wrong, make a guess.

Let's imagine you are taking a test in which each answer has four choices and you are penalized one fourth of a point for each wrong answer. If you have no clue and cannot eliminate any of the answer choices, you're better off leaving the question blank because the odds of answering correctly are one in four. This makes the penalty and the odds equal. However, if you can eliminate one of the choices, the odds are now in your favor. You have a one in three chance of answering the question correctly. Fortunately, few tests are scored using such elaborate means, but if your test is one of them, know the penalties and calculate your odds before you take a guess on a question.

If You Finish Early

Use any time you have left at the end of the test or test section to check your work. First, make certain you've put the answers in the right places. As you're doing this, make sure you've answered each question only once. Most standardized tests are scored in such a way that questions with more than one answer are marked wrong. If you've erased an answer, make sure you've done a good job. Check for stray marks on your answer sheet that could distort your score.

After you've checked for these obvious errors, take a second look at the more difficult questions. You've probably heard the folk wisdom about never changing an answer. It's not always good advice. If you have a good reason for thinking a response is wrong, change it.

AFTER THE TEST

Once you've finished, *congratulate yourself.* You've worked hard to prepare; now it's time to enjoy yourself and relax. Remember that celebration you planned before the test? Now it's time to go to it!

GOOD LUCK!

ANSWERS

1. The strongest support for Anderson's argument is **d,** a direct comparison of how much the city spends per year on these services and how much the city would save by farming the services out to private companies. Remember, Anderson's argument is that the city could save millions by giving these services over to the private sector, and this comparison would show exactly how much this city (not other cities) would save.

2. Answer **c** is most likely to work against Anderson's argument because it is the strongest evidence that the plan didn't work in similar cities. Furthermore, it shows that city councils that had approved similar plans had to reinstate public services due to citizen protests. Since city council members are elected officials, it's important for them to keep their constituents happy, and **c** suggests privatizing these services does not keep citizens happy. Furthermore, you should be able to see that **a, b,** and **d** are all reasons that would be likely to cause citizens to protest and demand a return to public services.

POST-TEST

I f you'd like to gauge how much your critical thinking and reasoning skills have improved from your work in this book, try this post-test. Though the questions are different from the pretest, the format is the same, so you will be able to directly compare test results. The only key difference between the two tests is that the post-test uses the vocabulary words you've learned throughout this book.

When you complete this test, grade yourself, and then compare your score with your score on the pretest. If your score now is much greater than your pretest score, congratulations—you've profited noticeably from your hard work. If your score shows little improvement, perhaps there are certain chapters you need to review. Do you notice a pattern to the types of questions you got wrong? Whatever you score on this post-test, keep this book around for review and to refer to when you need tips on reasoning skills.

There's an answer sheet you can use for filling in the correct answers on the next page. Or, if you prefer, simply circle the answer numbers in this book. If the book doesn't belong to you, write the numbers 1–35 on a piece of paper and record your answers there. Take as much time as you need to do this short test. When you finish, check your answers against the answer key that follows this test. Each answer tells you which lesson of this book teaches you about the reasoning strategy in that question.

Good luck!

1.	ⓐ	ⓑ	ⓒ	ⓓ
2.	ⓐ	ⓑ	ⓒ	ⓓ
3.	ⓐ	ⓑ	ⓒ	ⓓ
4.	ⓐ	ⓑ	ⓒ	ⓓ
5.	ⓐ	ⓑ	ⓒ	ⓓ
6.	ⓐ	ⓑ	ⓒ	ⓓ
7.	ⓐ	ⓑ	ⓒ	ⓓ
8.	ⓐ	ⓑ	ⓒ	ⓓ
9.	ⓐ	ⓑ	ⓒ	ⓓ
10.	ⓐ	ⓑ	ⓒ	ⓓ
11.	ⓐ	ⓑ	ⓒ	ⓓ
12.	ⓐ	ⓑ	ⓒ	ⓓ
13.	ⓐ	ⓑ	ⓒ	ⓓ
14.	ⓐ	ⓑ	ⓒ	ⓓ
15.	ⓐ	ⓑ	ⓒ	ⓓ

16.	ⓐ	ⓑ	ⓒ	ⓓ
17.	ⓐ	ⓑ	ⓒ	ⓓ
18.	ⓐ	ⓑ	ⓒ	ⓓ
19.	ⓐ	ⓑ	ⓒ	ⓓ
20.	ⓐ	ⓑ	ⓒ	ⓓ
21.	ⓐ	ⓑ	ⓒ	ⓓ
22.	ⓐ	ⓑ	ⓒ	ⓓ
23.	ⓐ	ⓑ	ⓒ	ⓓ
24.	ⓐ	ⓑ	ⓒ	ⓓ
25.	ⓐ	ⓑ	ⓒ	ⓓ
26.	ⓐ	ⓑ	ⓒ	ⓓ
27.	ⓐ	ⓑ	ⓒ	ⓓ
28.	ⓐ	ⓑ	ⓒ	ⓓ
29.	ⓐ	ⓑ	ⓒ	ⓓ
30.	ⓐ	ⓑ	ⓒ	ⓓ

31.	ⓐ	ⓑ	ⓒ	ⓓ
32.	ⓐ	ⓑ	ⓒ	ⓓ
33.	ⓐ	ⓑ	ⓒ	ⓓ
34.	ⓐ	ⓑ	ⓒ	ⓓ
35.	ⓐ	ⓑ	ⓒ	ⓓ

POST-TEST

Read the following passage and then answer the questions that follow.

Joshua's 10-year-old stereo system has just died. He wants to buy a new one, but isn't sure what kind to get. He's on a tight budget but wants good quality – something that will last him for years. He has a large tape collection but for the last several months he's only bought CDs because he believes the quality is much better.

1. Which of the following most accurately presents the issues Joshua must consider, in order of priority?
   a. cost, quality, and brand name of system
   b. quality, cost, and components of system
   c. components, quality, and warranty for system
   d. trade-in value of old system and components of new system

2. Which of the following is probably the best choice for Joshua?
   a. a medium-quality stereo with CD player but no tape deck, regular price
   b. a high-quality stereo with a tape deck but no CD, regular price
   c. a high-quality stereo with CD player but no tape deck on sale for half price
   d. a low-quality stereo with CD player and tape deck, sale price

Choose the best answer for each of the following.

3. "These are the most beautiful paintings in the entire museum" is
   a. a fact
   b. an opinion
   c. a tentative truth
   d. none of the above

4. "The Liberty Bell has three cracks in it" is
   a. a fact
   b. an opinion
   c. a tentative truth
   d. none of the above

What, if anything, is wrong with the following passages?

5. "He's been known to embellish the truth on occasion."
   a. "Embellish the truth" is a euphemism.
   b. "Embellish the truth" is a dysphemism.
   c. "On occasion" is vague.
   d. There's nothing wrong with this sentence.

6. "Do you support the ban of nuclear and biological weapons that would leave us defenseless against those countries that will continue to build nuclear and biological warheads in secret?"
a. The question uses a euphemism.
b. The question uses a dysphemism.
c. The question is loaded or biased.
d. There's nothing wrong with this question.

7. "Give her a chance, Carl. She's a good person, and she's had a really hard time since her mother died. She's never worked in an office before, but you'll be giving her the first break she's had in a long time."
a. The speaker is using peer pressure.
b. The speaker is appealing to Carl's sense of pity.
c. The speaker is using a red herring.
d. There's nothing wrong with this passage.

8. "What does he know? He's a Republican."
a. The speaker is presenting a straw man.
b. The speaker is asking a loaded question.
c. The speaker is presenting an *ad hominem* argument.
d. There's nothing wrong with this passage.

9. "Tough-Scrub is tougher on dirt!"
a. The ad is making an incomplete claim.
b. The ad is appealing to our vanity.
c. The claim the ad makes is untestable.
d. There's nothing wrong with this ad.

10. "None of us are going to vote to make the employee lounge a non-smoking area, so neither are you, right?"
a. The speaker is presenting a no in-betweens argument.
b. The speaker is using circular reasoning.
c. The speaker is using peer pressure.
d. There's nothing wrong with this passage.

11. "I was going so fast, Officer, because I was in a hurry."
a. The speaker is appealing to vanity.
b. The speaker is using circular reasoning.
c. The speaker is reversing cause and effect.
d. There's nothing wrong with this passage.

12. "The average employee works only 45 hours a week and takes home $65,000 a year in salary. Not bad, eh?"
a. The speaker has made a hasty generalization.
b. The speaker has committed a *non sequitur*.
c. The speaker's use of averages could be misleading.
d. There's nothing wrong with this passage.

13. "If you have sinus trouble, you should try acupuncture. I had sinus troubles for years, and since I've been going to the acupuncturist for the last six months, I can breathe better, sleep better, and I have more energy. And it's painless."
a. The speaker is using peer pressure.
b. The speaker is presenting a circular explanation.
c. The speaker is making a hasty generalization.
d. There's nothing wrong with this passage.

14. "So the end result is that we either have to cut jobs or go out of business."
   a. The speaker has presented a no in-betweens fallacy.
   b. The speaker has presented a straw man.
   c. The speaker has presented a slippery slope scenario.
   d. There's nothing wrong with this passage.

15. "Music is based on numbers. I'm good with numbers, so I'd be a good musician."
   a. The speaker has committed a *non sequitur*.
   b. The speaker has committed an *ad hominem* fallacy.
   c. The speaker has made a hasty generalization.
   d. There's nothing wrong with this passage.

16. "The only thing those animal rights people want to do is make you believe that a monkey has all the same rights as a human being."
   a. The speaker is presenting a no in-betweens situation.
   b. The speaker is presenting a straw man.
   c. The speaker is using scare tactics.
   d. There's nothing wrong with this passage.

17. "I have succeeded because I was destined to succeed."
   a. The speaker is presenting a circular explanation.
   b. The speaker is presenting an untestable explanation.
   c. The speaker is reversing cause and effect.
   d. There's nothing wrong with this passage.

18. "If you start smoking cigarettes, next thing you know you'll be smoking marijuana, and then before you know it you'll be addicted to crack."
   a. The speaker is making a biased generalization.
   b. The speaker is presenting a *post hoc, ergo propter hoc* fallacy.
   c. The speaker is presenting a slippery slope argument.
   d. There's nothing wrong with this passage.

19. "I know you're concerned about whether or not I inappropriately allocated funds. But what you really should be worrying about is what Senator Hinckley is doing with his illegal campaign contributions!"
   a. The speaker is presenting a red herring.
   b. The speaker is committing an *ad hominem*.
   c. The speaker is using peer pressure.
   d. There's nothing wrong with this passage.

20. "Hey, Jim, have you gotten the new Pearl Jam album yet? I heard one song on the radio and it's awesome! This is their best album yet!"
   a. The speaker presents a circular explanation.
   b. The speaker is making a hasty generalization.
   c. The speaker is committing the *post hoc, ergo propter hoc* fallacy.
   d. There's nothing wrong with this passage.

In the following situations, which source is most credible?

21. You want to find out about the condition of a used pick-up truck you're thinking of buying.
a. the truck's owner
b. a friend who refurbishes used cars and trucks
c. a used car salesman
d. an independent garage mechanic

22. You want to find out about the quality of goods in an antique store.
a. a friend who shops there all the time
b. the store's owner
c. an antique specialist
d. a local historian

Read the following argument carefully and answer the questions that follow.

(1) School should be in session year-round rather than just September through June. (2) Having the summer months off means that children spend the first two months reviewing what they learned the year before. (3) This is a waste of precious time. (4) Imagine how much more children would learn if they had an extra four months a year to learn new material. (5) In addition, with so many single-parent households and families where both parents have to work, child care in the long summer months is a serious financial burden on families. (6) Those who can't afford child care have no choice but to leave their children alone.

23. What is the main point (conclusion) of the argument?
a. sentence 1
b. sentence 2
c. sentence 3
d. sentence 4
e. sentence 5

24. This conclusion is
a. a fact
b. an opinion
c. a tentative truth

25. How many major premises support this conclusion?
a. one
b. two
c. three
d. four

26. Which of the following would most strengthen this argument?
a. "Teachers across the country agree."
b. "According to a *New York Times* survey, just one week of summertime child care costs an average of $250."
c. "At least we should make summer camps more affordable and educational."
d. "Studies show that children who read throughout the summer do better in the next school year."

27. Sentence 6 commits which of the following fallacies?
  a. red herring
  b. straw man
  c. no in-betweens
  d. *non sequitur*

Read the following passages carefully and answer the questions that follow.

Every day for the last six weeks, LeeAnne has been doing yoga before work in the morning. Since then, she has noticed that she is more relaxed. She has also been given an award for her dedication at work and been asked out on several dates. Furthermore, she has noticed an increase in her appetite.

28. Which of the following is very likely to be the result of her yoga?
  a. that she is more relaxed
  b. that she is being asked out on dates
  c. that she has gotten an award at work
  d. **a** and **c**

29. If LeeAnne were to claim that her social life has improved because of her yoga, which of the following would be true?
  a. She'd be making a hasty generalization.
  b. She'd be committing the *post hoc, ergo propter hoc* fallacy.
  c. She'd be reversing cause and effect.
  d. She wouldn't be committing any logical fallacies.

Rhonda wants to plant a flower garden in her yard. She knows she needs to do each of the following:
  1. Decide which flowers she likes best
  2. Find out which flowers grow best in her climate
  3. Buy gardening equipment
  4. Design the flower garden

30. In which order should Rhonda take the steps listed above?
  a. 1, 2, 3, 4
  b. 4, 3, 2, 1
  c. 2, 1, 3, 4
  d. 2, 1, 4, 3

You would like to find out whether burglary has increased or decreased in your area since the new low-income housing developments went up in your neighborhood. You get the crime reports for the last ten years and compare them. You see that there has indeed been a dramatic increase in the number of burglaries in the last five years.

31. For which of the following reasons is your comparison invalid?
  a. Your comparison doesn't consider who committed those burglaries.
  b. Your comparison doesn't take into consideration the changes in population size during that time period.
  c. Your comparison doesn't consider that the police department may have revised its definition of "burglary" in the last ten years.
  d. both **a** and **c**
  e. both **b** and **c**

32. Which of the following could you logically conclude from your comparison?
   a. The increase in population is probably the chief cause of any increase in the number of burglaries.
   b. People from low-income families are more likely to commit burglaries than middle-class people.
   c. The number of burglaries in a given area is likely to rise when the police force is reduced.
   d. The overall lack of morals in people today is probably the chief cause of any increase in the number of burglaries.

33. If you were to survey people in your neighborhood about crime, which approach would be most likely to get you the most accurate results?
   a. surveying people who've lived in your neighborhood for at least ten years
   b. surveying people who've lived in your neighborhood for less than five years
   c. surveying random people shopping at Bloomingdale's
   d. surveying random people at the neighborhood's two grocery stores

Michelle has a list of chores she needs to get done before 5:00. She needs to vacuum, but she can't do that between 10–12 or 2–4 because the baby will be sleeping. She needs to do yesterday's dishes, but she can't do that between 9–10 or 12–1 because she and the baby will be eating. She needs to cook dinner, but she can't do that until she does yesterday's dishes, and she wants to do that as close to dinnertime as possible. She also needs to dust, but she wants to do that before she vacuums.

34. Which of the following is the best schedule for Michelle?

	10:00–12:00	1:00–2:00	2:00–4:00	4:00–5:00
a.	vacuum	dust	cook	dishes
b.	dust	vacuum	dishes	cook
c.	dust	dishes	vacuum	cook
d.	dishes	cook	dust	vacuum

Brenda is hosting a dinner party. On one side of the table, Ed (E) is sitting next to Mary (M). There are two seats between Annabelle (A) and Mary. Annabelle is next to Carl (C). Carl is one seat away from Mary. Roger (R) is at one end of the table.

35. In which order are these guests sitting?
   a. R, A, C, E, M
   b. R, C, M, E, A
   c. E, M, A, C, R
   d. M, C, R, A, E

ANSWER KEY

If you miss any of the answers, you can find help for that kind of question in the lesson shown to the right of the answer.

1. b. Lesson 2
2. c. Lesson 2
3. b. Lesson 3
4. c. Lesson 3
5. a. Lesson 5
6. c. Lesson 5
7. b. Lesson 11
8. c. Lesson 13
9. a. Lesson 7
10. c. Lesson 11
11. b. Lesson 12
12. c. Lesson 7
13. d. Lesson 6–9
14. a. Lesson 12
15. a. Lessons 15, 16
16. b. Lesson 13
17. a. Lesson 14
18. c. Lesson 12

19. a. Lesson 13
20. b. Lessons 15, 16
21. d. Lesson 4
22. c. Lesson 4
23. a. Lesson 6
24. b. Lesson 3
25. b. Lesson 6
26. b. Lessons 6–9
27. c. Lesson 12
28. a. Lessons 15, 17
29. b. Lesson 17
30. d. Lessons 2, 20
31. e. Lessons 15, 18, 20
32. a. Lessons 15, 18, 20
33. d. Lesson 18
34. b. Lessons 15, 20
35. a. Lessons 15, 20

A·P·P·E·N·D·I·X
ADDITIONAL RESOURCES

If this book has inspired you to continue to improve your reasoning and critical thinking skills, take a look at the list below for suggested further reading. The topics covered in these books range from argumentation and debate to solving logic puzzles. Remember, reasoning skills are vital for success in all areas of life. The process of acquiring and developing these skills should be lifelong.

SUGGESTED READING

- Barry, Vincent E. *Critical Edge: Critical Thinking for Reading and Writing.* Harcourt, 1992.

- Bierman, Arthur K., and R. N. Assali. *The Critical Thinking Handbook.* Prentice Hall, 1995.

- Browne, M. Neil, and Stuart M. Keeley. *Asking the Right Questions: A Guide to Critical Thinking.* Prentice Hall, 1997.

- Capaldi, Nicholas. *The Art of Deception: How to Win an Argument, Defend a Case, Recognize a Fallacy, See Through Deception, Persuade a Skeptic, Turn Defeat into Victory.* Prometheus Books, 1996.

- Cederblom, Jerry, and David W. Paulsen. *Critical Reasoning: Understanding and Criticizing Arguments and Theories.* Wadsworth, 1996.

- Diestler, Sherry. *Becoming a Critical Thinker: A User-Friendly Manual.* Prentice Hall, 1997.

- Dispezio, Michael A. *Challenging Critical Thinking Puzzles.* Sterling Publications, 1998.

- Dispezio, Michael A. *Critical Thinking Puzzles.* Sterling Publications, 1996.

- Dispezio, Michael A. *Great Critical Thinking Puzzles.* Sterling Publications, 1997.

- Edwards, Ronald. *Problem Solving Through Critical Thinking.* Addison-Wesley, 1993.

- Fearnside, W. Ward. *About Thinking.* Prentice Hall, 1996.

- Freeley, Austin J. *Argumentation and Debate: Critical Thinking for Reasoned Decision Making.* Wadsworth, 1997.

- Gibson, Paula, and Marcia L. Laskey. *College Study Strategies: Thinking and Learning.* Allyn & Bacon, 1996.

- Gilovich, Thomas. *How We Know What Isn't So: The Fallibility of Human Reason in Everyday Life.* Free Press, 1993.

- Halpern, Diane. *Thought and Knowledge: An Introduction to Critical Thinking.* Lawrence Erlbaum, 1996.

- Inch, Edward, and Barbara Warnick. *Critical Thinking and Communication: The Use of Reason in Argument.* Allyn & Bacon, 1997.

- Kiersky, James Hugh, and Nicholas J. Caste. *Thinking Critically: Techniques for Logical Reasoning.* West/Wadsworth, 1994.

- Leblanc, Jill. *Thinking Clearly: A Guide to Critical Reasoning.* Norton, 1998.

- Little, Linda W. *Problem Solving: Critical Thinking and Communication Skills.* Longman, 1991.

- Longman, Debbie Guice, Rhonda Holt Atkinson, and Julie Ann Breeden. *Strategic Thinking and Reading.* West/Wadsworth, 1997.

- Mayfield, Marlys. *Thinking for Yourself: Developing Critical Thinking Skills Through Reading and Writing.* Wadsworth, 1996.

- Meltzer, Marilyn, and Susan Marcus Palau. *Acquiring Critical Thinking Skills.* W. B. Saunders, 1996.

- Missimer, C. A. *Good Arguments: An Introduction to Critical Thinking.* Prentice Hall, 1994.

- Moore, Brooke Noel, and Richard Parker. *Critical Thinking.* Mayfield, 1998.

- Parlette, Snowden. *The Brain Workout Book.* M. Evans, 1997.

- Paustian, Anthony. *Imagine! Enhancing Your Problem-Solving and Critical Thinking Skills.* Prentice Hall, 1996.

- Romain, Dianne. *Thinking Things Through: Critical Thinking for Decisions We Can Live With.* Mayfield, 1996.

- Ruchlis, Hy. *Clear Thinking: A Practical Introduction.* Prometheus Books, *1990.*

- Ruggiero, Vincent Ryan. *The Art of Thinking: A Guide to Critical and Creative Thought.* Longman, 1997.

- Ruggiero, Vincent Ryan. *Beyond Feelings: A Guide to Critical Thinking.* Mayfield, 1997.

- Salmon, Merrilee. *Introduction to Logic and Critical Thinking.* Harcourt, 1994.

- Vos Savant, Marilyn. *The Power of Logical Thinking: Easy Lessons in the Art of Reasoning . . . And Hard Facts about Its Absence in Our Lives.* St. Martin's Press, 1997.

NOTES

NOTES

NOTES

NOTES